Jeffrey L. Kuhlman is an experienced educator and has worked internationally for many years as an educator, business owner, and ship's master. As both captain and educator, his three years working in Africa, three years in India, a year in South Korea, a year in the Persian Gulf, mission work up the Amazon and elsewhere in Brazil, and training in Chile has provided him with a global view of the human spirit and in-depth experience with personal development and communication.

As an Education Consultant and Student Learning Advocate, he is a member of "The Kuhlmans" teaching and presentation team under the name "Classroom CPR". He currently speaks to and trains education professionals in classroom management and differentiated learning.

Jeffrey Kuhlman has written for several trade magazines and spoken to professional organizations domestically and internationally on the topics of Best Practices in Maritime Security and Defense Training, Disaster and Emergency Management, and Training the Trainer. Prior to his civilian career at sea, he was a licensed History teacher in New Jersey and taught language in the Republic of South Korea. Kuhlman has recently retired as an Adjunct Instructor at Nova Southeastern University. He has written curriculum for and taught the Maritime Track for a Master's Degree in Disaster and Emergency Preparedness at Nova Southeastern University, Florida.

Kuhlman is proud to have honorably worn the uniforms of the U.S. Navy, U.S. Marine Corps, and Army National Guard. His combat experience was as a field Hospital Corpsman assigned to the Eleventh Marine Regiment, First Marine Division, Republic of South Vietnam. Other assignments included Medical Deep Sea Diving Technician / First Class Diver, Gunner's Mate Guns, and Cannon Crewman. He originated the Warren County Arts Association in Warren County, New Jersey, and authored a number of books about maritime security and defense and education.

Certain people in an author's life prove pivotal in his or her development and wellbeing. For me that person is my wife, Glenna. She has steadfastly stood next to me through many of the experiences that made this book possible and my life both full and completely happy. Even through difficult periods, she has proven to be my sturdy rampart. As an educator of fine reputation, she will appreciate this book and its heartfelt dedication.

Thank you, my dear.

Your Jeff.

Jeffrey L. Kuhlman

CREATE A GREAT HOMESCHOOL EXPERIENCE

LEARN TO TEACH IN YOUR HOME FOR YOUR CHILD'S SUCCESS

AUSTIN MACAULEY PUBLISHERS™

LONDON • CAMBRIDGE • NEW YORK • SHARJAH

Ordering Information:
Quantity sales: special discounts are available on quantity purchases by corporations, associations, and others. For details, contact the publisher at the address below.

Publisher's Cataloging-in-Publication data
Kuhlman, Jeffrey L.
Create a Great Homeschool Experience: Learn to Teach in Your Home for Your Child's Success

ISBN 9781641828420 (Paperback)
ISBN 9781641828437 (Hardback)
ISBN 9781645366232 (ePub e-book)

Library of Congress Control Number: 2019939462

The main category of the book — Education/ Home Schooling

www.austinmacauley.com/us

First Published (2019)
Austin Macauley Publishers LLC
40 Wall Street, 28th Floor
New York, NY 10005
USA

mail-usa@austinmacauley.com
+1 (646) 5125767

Books are seldom written in a vacuum. The writing requires moral and practical support as well as sharing the experiences expressed in the text. There are many people who have provided this support, but two deserve special thanks. They are my wife, Glenna, and my grandson, Scott, without whom I could not have written this book.

I thank my wife, my colleague and dedicated proofreader of the reams of paper I generate, for the support she has provided me, even when she was tired, bored, ill, or healthy. She was always dependably there in her support of my efforts. She has been a Presidential Award-winning educator for Excellence in Teaching Elementary Mathematics in the State of New Jersey. She is listed in the *Who's Who of American Teachers,* but her background provides so much more in courage, care, and love. An educator, private pilot, a test pilot for the paraplane, commercial mariner after retiring from the classroom, deacon and elder of our church, occasional missionary, and successful hunter of meat for African farm workers, she has become a model for so many including me.

I also thank our grandson, Scott Tirpok, without whom we would not have had the shared experience in homeschooling necessary for this book. Scott spent his ninth-grade school year homeschooling with Glenna and me on our forty-five-foot ketch as we sailed from New England to Florida with a trip to Port Lucaya in The Bahamas. He was often a difficult student. When he arrived on board, he had been a teenager without boundaries, trapped in a maelstrom of well-intended special-education student programs.

A year later, he found himself back home, again attending his homeschool, but now an honor-roll student who had accepted good boundaries and established a mature work ethic. Now, many years later, he has met his personal goal of becoming a professional power company lineman, today working to restore power in Puerto Rico following this year's hurricanes. He has planned well for his future. He is a true success story, mature, and happy. Congratulations, Grandson!

Table of Contents

Foreword

Having had a successful experience in homeschooling our grandson, Scott, I have often found myself in many discussions about the efficacy of homeschooling. Education professionals are split on the merits of homeschooling with the greater number less than supportive. Few seem to have much direct knowledge on thess topic however, and their comparison is usually with a dedicated classroom student experience. Parents are usually interested in providing their child a successful home-schooling experience by being at the same time fearful of accepting the challenge, not knowing how to begin due to their perceived ignorance of the educational experience and lack of topical knowledge.

It is for those parents interested in homeschooling that this book has been written. It is my intent to provide a guide, for gaining adequate general knowledge of homeschooling, to those parents so that they are armed with the information necessary for them to confidently decide whether to home-school or not. If they choose to school their student at home, they will find here a guide suitable to get them started and established.

As a parent, I found that many educators, especially in administrative positions, tend to be elitist in their knowledge of education as related to the politics of the day. I often found the attitude "I know something you don't" demeanor of some educators to be inconsiderate at best. I also determined through conversations that I was not alone. If their children are in traditional classrooms, the contents of this book will provide parents with important information to assist them in communicating directly to members of the education institution.

Today, as an educator myself, I hope to help resolve some of the information misunderstandings between parents and educators and to help alleviate the fears of parents interested in homeschooling as the education of students at home has proven immensely successful, giving students more options to attain their own success. My opinions expressed in this book are derived from my experiences, learned knowledge, observations, and research. The opinions of others are appropriately identified.

Chapter 1
Let's Begin

If you are a parent, grandparent, guardian, or anyone who takes on the responsibility of educating a child or teen, your first determiner is to whom you should listen for accurate information. It is the intention of this book to provide that information to you and to provide you with a primmer that will help you learn and grow into an effective home-school teacher.

I am writing this book in the first and second person as it is not an academic treatise but a conversation between you and me. You may exchange the singular, I/me to the plural we, if you like, since such guides as this incorporate facts, ideas, and input from various sources that include colleagues, associates. In my case, it includes my wife Glenna too, who is a Presidential Award-winning educator with over thirty-seven years' experience in the elementary classroom, teaching mathematics and teaching methods to her fellow teachers.

Since this book is intended to be conversational, you may contact me at info@marisector.com or visit my websites at www.cpr4classroommanagement.com, www.rwt2015.com, or www.marisector.com. To avoid the confusion of gender in grammar, we assume that all "he's" and "she's" when referring to students or teachers is gender neutral and both, he and she, will be used alternately in the text.

As an educator, the first comment I hear when discussing homeschooling with a parent is, 'I don't know how.'

The next comment is the question, 'How do I begin?'

Of course, the question is answered first. 'You have just begun.'

By the time you have asked this question, you have already considered homeschooling and probably have talked to several people and read many articles. Enough so that you are relatively sure you wish to pursue homeschooling information in greater depth.

Your Rewards

There are many rewards for you once you have accepted the home-school challenge. Remember that homeschooling for you is truly an exercise in consistency and organization. You can consider this as a construct that has the greatest of purposes, setting the foundation for a student's life. What he or she will learn from you will relate directly to how that student refers to his other world from that time forward.

My wife Glenna and I are both educators. She is a Presidential Award winner for Excellence in Teaching Elementary Mathematics in the State of New Jersey in 1994. I write the curriculum for and teach in an award-winning Master of Science in Disaster and Emergency Management degree program as being one of the ten best in the country.

Even though we are experienced and winning educators, we home-schooled our grandson, Scott, and contended with all those same concerns as you. We were successful; Scott has reached all his short-term goals and is now working on his long-term life goals. I will use Scott as an example from time-to-time in this book. Scott's success is an example of the rewards we, as will you, receive.

As a home-school teacher, you will have the opportunity to establish, re-establish, and strengthen your relationship with your student. Home-school parents can become mentors as well as teachers. A teacher provides information while a mentor helps the student apply and internalize that information. In a home-school environment, you will have the opportunity to enjoy both.

An important reward is the fact that your experiences and anecdotes will furnish your student with experiences her few years of life would not have provided. She can learn from your mistakes and take advantage of your solutions. Likewise, she can copy and repeat your decisions, actions, and pursuits that were successful so that she will have a foundation for accomplishments of her own.

There are many reasons to homeschool. Among these is making a safer learning environment that is found in many public schools. In addition to this, the home-school parent can provide a better social, ethical, belief, and value system than is possible in public venues. It is true that our youth make their decisions based primarily on emotional foundations with only their limited few years of protected experience to guide their way. Along these lines, the home-schooled student's social interactions can be more effectively guided.

It isn't among the least of your rewards that you will gain a greater appreciation of patience and the proper application of discipline and boundary building. Our Scott was especially challenging in this area as he had grown up in an environment in which he had few boundaries other than those he established for himself. To his credit, he did not steal, intentionally hurt others, or fall into the trap of drug use and addiction, as did another in his family.

As an example of consistency in the application of boundaries, I give you an example from my family. Glenna and I home-schooled our grandson on our 45-foot ketch, a very sound sailing vessel. As his school year had come to an end, we sailed from Fort Lauderdale and stopped for a couple of days in Port Lucaya in The Bahamas where we came across a few teenagers that were also in liveaboard families. Glenna and I decided that we would stay an extra day to give Scott some teen socialization time as a special treat for Scott's work well done.

As we left to a town for some shopping, we told Scott that he could spend time with his sailing friends, but return to the boat by 10:00 P.M. Naturally, he agreed. We arrived at the boat about 9:30 P.M. and no Scott. There was no Scott at 10:00, or again at 10:30; our search began. We knew the teenagers would be together. We found Scott about 11:00 P.M. lounging with the other teens in a hot tub at a local resort.

The sailing community tends to be close-knit; but we were naturally concerned about his welfare and felt it important to be consistent in our application of his boundaries. A ninth grader does not have the experience or knowledge necessary to make or apply his own boundaries in an unfamiliar country, even though we were with our sailing community. We were happy that he was safe. However, since he disobeyed, he had to follow our boundary rule, which stated that he had to stay aboard the next day cleaning the topside of the boat and helping with readying the boat for departure. Instead of being able to enjoy the day with his friends, he worked (doing essential things, not busy-work), and we spent time in the local village, checking on him periodically.

That was the last time he "tried" us. Not a happy camper, but he understood his error and his consequences because we had negotiated the aspects earlier. In regards to the establishment of boundaries, we had enforced our home-school boundaries and reinforced an ethical standard. Scott held himself accountable for his decision to stay out rather than being on the boat where he should have been. Lessons, such as these, are only possible in a home-schooled environment. This was a great reward for us because our student had had few boundaries before his homeschooling.

The Student's Rewards:
The home-schooled student has more evident rewards. The first great reward is his greater involvement in his particular learning process. Being taught on a one-on-one or a two-on-one basis with closer relationship building as part of the process, the student begins to help construct his personal learning plan and boundaries.

The home-school student will feel the thrill of succeeding in his academics. Successes such as these are foundational to establishing the self-esteem necessary for a rich life. Moreover, the homeschooler will benefit from a course structure constructed to meet his needs and not those in a one-size-fits-all conception often found in public schools.

The home-schooled student will gain a feeling of self-worth and confidence as he begins his new life, either in work or in advanced collegial studies.

With greater self-esteem and confidence, her social development would probably allow for better choices in friends, acquaintances, and workplace relationships than most non-homeschoolers. This would be expected to include a choice of spouse and other essential relationships.

There is a myriad of other more positive results, including better and more enjoyable career choices, higher-income potential, and greater social access.

Good words, right? But, what do other experts say?

Statistics
There is much data out there about home-schooling statistics and they are very consistent with their results. We searched several well-respected resources; their findings follow.

The [1]Home School Legal Defense Association has parsed the results in many studies and put them together in their article, Academic Statistics on Home Schooling. They include:

'In 1997, a study of 5,402 homeschool students from 1,657 families was released. It was entitled "Strengths of Their Own: Home Schoolers across America". The study demonstrated that homeschoolers, on the average, out-performed their counterparts in the public schools by 30 to 37 percentile points in all subjects. A significant finding when analyzing the data for 8th graders was the evidence that homeschoolers who are homeschooled two or more years score substantially higher than students who have been homeschooled one year or less. The new homeschoolers were scoring on the average in the 59th percentile compared to students homeschooled the last two or more years who scored between 86th and 92nd percentile.' Dr. Brian Ray (2004)

Not only do homeschoolers tend to show better test scores but also the longer they are homeschooled, the wider the performance separation is between homeschooling and public schooling. In 1998, Dr. Lawrence Radnor confirmed these findings.

This was confirmed in another study by Dr. Lawrence Rudner of 20,760 homeschooled students, which found the homeschoolers who have homeschooled all their school aged years had the highest academic achievement. This was especially apparent in the higher grades. This is a good encouragement to families catch the long-range vision and homeschool through high school. Dr. Lawrence Rudner, (1998)

---

[1] Home School Legal Defense Association, Legal Research Supplement, Academic Statistics on Homeschooling, J. Michael Smith and Michael P. Farris, October 22, 2004

It has also been found that race was NOT a determining factor in the success of homeschoolers. Strengths of Their Own: Home Schoolers across America stated:

[2]These findings show that when parents, regardless of race, commit themselves to make the necessary sacrifices and tutor their children at home, almost all obstacles present in other school systems disappear, Michael Smith and Michael P. Farris, (2004)

Economic consideration had often been pointed to as a measure of educational quality. This fallacious concept was brought to light in Dr. Lawrence Radnor's 1998 paper.

[3]Another obstacle that seems to be overcome in homeschooling is the need to spend a great deal of money in order to have a good education. In 'Strengths of Their Own', Dr. Ray found the average cost per home-school student is $546 while the average cost per public school student is $5,325. Yet the home-school children in this study averaged in 85th percentile while the public-school students averaged in the 50th percentile on nationally standardized achievement tests.

'Similarly, the 1998 study by Dr. Rudner of 20,760 students found that eighth-grade students whose parents spend $199 or less on their home education score, on the average, in the 80th percentile. Eighth-grade students whose parents spend $400 to $599 on their home education also score on the average, in the 80th percentile! Once the parents spend over $600, the students do slightly better, scoring in the 83rd percentile.' J. Michael Smith and Michael P. Farris, (2004)

---

[2] Home School Legal Defense Association, Legal Research Supplement, Academic Statistics on Homeschooling, J. Michael Smith and Michael P. Farris, October 22, 2004
[3] Home School Legal Defense Association, Legal Research Supplement, Academic Statistics on Homeschooling, J. Michael Smith and Michael P. Farris, October 22, 2004

Clearly, the amount of money spent per student has no bearing on the success of the student. In fact, homeschooling is perhaps the least-expensive schooling with the best results.

As we continue through our statistical morass, we should note that when you see the term percentile, this has little to do with a subject's test scores. It has everything to do with the standing within a group of students. An 85 percent score provides a numerical grade for the results of the test. An 85 percentile, on the other hand, indicates that the student has tested as being in the top 15 percent of all students in that group, which could include many 85% grade-scores. With our hypothetical 85 percentile, 84 percent of that group of students scored lower grades. A percentile score is not the same as an individual student's percentage score.

[4]The Bob Jones University Testing Service of South Carolina provided test results of Montana homeschoolers. Also, a survey of homeschoolers in Montana was conducted by the National Home Education Research Institute.
Dr. Brian Ray (2016) evaluated the survey and test results, and found:
On average, the home education students in this study scored above the national norm in all subject areas on standardized achievement tests. These students scored, on average, at the 72nd percentile in terms of a combination of their reading, language, and math performance. This is well above the national average.

According to the National Home Education Research Institute, Facts on Homeschooling, the following statistics are important indicators of the success and subsequent growth of homeschooling in America.[5]

---

[4] The Bob Jones University Testing Service of South Carolina
[5] Research Facts on Homeschooling, Brian D. Ray PhD., March 23, 2016, National Home Education Research Institute.

Note the difference in the taxpayer cost figures between the 1995 reference and the following 2016 reference. This difference indicates that the cost increases to the taxpayer are exponential.

- Once an education alternative, homeschooling is becoming mainstream.
- People from all demographics are beginning to homeschool regardless of age, economic standing, race, religion, or ethnic background.
- There are now over 2.3 million homeschool students in the U.S., up from 2.0 million in 2010 indicating a 2–8% growth rate.
- Homeschool families are generally not dependent on public funds and the local taxpayers do not have to pay for the homeschooler's education. Homeschoolers spend over $27 million in education costs that taxpayers do not need to pay.
- While taxpayers spend about $11,700 per year per student, homeschooling families pay only about $600/year.
- Homeschoolers generally perform 15–30 percentile point better than public schools.
- They score better on SAT and ACT scores than public school students. These are the scores looked at and often required by colleges and universities.
- It makes no difference whether the homeschool parents were professional teachers or not.
- Homeschooled students are often regularly engaged in social activities outside their home and typically do more public service volunteering than other students.
- They tend to vote and attend public meetings more often.
- They succeed at college at a much higher rate.

[6]Bright Hub Education in Homeschooling Statistics: What Research Reveals about Homeschooling by Laura Powell, 2014, confirms that up to 2.4 million students were homeschooled in 2008 vs. 56.1 million in public schools. She interviewed 7,306 survey participants about their reasons for homeschooling. The results follow:

- 79.5% believed they could give their child a better education at home;
- 76.7% indicated religious reasons;
- 73.5% to teach their child values and beliefs;
- 69.2% to develop character and morality
- 66.7% object to what public schools teach; and
- 56.1% cite a poor learning environment in public schools.

I am not presenting these statistics and information to degrade public schools. Instead, since this is a book about homeschooling, we are presenting information useful to the potential home-school parent.

I am a public-school graduate. In my own case, it is fortunate that I am a reasonably bright individual, as I had some highly competent teachers. But sadly, some were among the poorest. I often found that I was relegated to figuring out the topical information myself. Although I went out for wrestling, football, and track teams, plus played summer soccer, I was not a popular or highly social person. Although I was kind and had a highly developed sense of ethics, I found little of value in on-campus socialization. Instead, I had to contend with bullying, always one against five or six odds and found myself defending others less capable of resistance than I.

I would have relished the opportunity for homeschooling, but homeschooling was not the option in the 1950s as it is

---

[6]   Homeschool   Statistics: What   Research   Reveals   About Homeschooling, Laura Powell, 5/15/2014, Bright Hub Education

nowadays. As an educator today, I can see the teaching deficiencies with which I had to contend. At that time, such vision was impossible, even though my parents were well educated.

Homeschool or not, it is an answer that is up to you. Homeschooling is not for everyone, but it is becoming more sophisticated each year. Hopefully, this book will help you understand the finer points of effective homeschool teaching.

Self-Assessment Questionnaire

Did you read the entire chapter? Yes ☐ No ☐

List three things you got out of the chapter:

1.

2.

3.

How will you apply these things to teaching your student?

Congratulations on completing this chapter!

Chapter 2
The Homeschool Environment

We have touched upon the question as to why we might want to homeschool. Once you make that decision, we should consider the student you will be teaching since his or her needs will determine what your teaching and her learning environment will be. Students come in all personalities, sizes,  shapes, perceptions, likes, dislikes, and all manner of differences found in any group of humans and all within the same family. Therefore, you must take care in how you establish an adequate, and hopefully effective, learning environment.

There is no average child. Although people frequently refer to norms, they most often intend "mean", which is only a mathematical average. To be sure, all students have the potential to be headaches, they are human with faults, the frailties and strengths. These are the factors that sometimes make teaching difficult. However, although means and averages may make a difference in statistical studies, these are our children and attending to their individualism is essential.

Let's look at two types of students that are often considered to be on opposite sides of the learning spectrum. Both require different responses for students with divergent needs. The first type of student we will discuss is the talented or gifted student. She may have a single or multiple talents and/or capabilities. At times, this may include autistic children or savants. At other times, these students have other or additional special needs considerations.

When we make our decision to homeschool, it is best to consider it as a long-term approach to education. As we have seen, statistics show that the longer a student is homeschooled the greater his success. This is important as in our homeschooling, we must formulate a sequence or foundation of learning that may not have occurred in an earlier public-school experience. This is not necessarily a fault in the public-school system but may be merely a result of need vs. resources. Looking at the 2+million homeschool children in the U.S. vs. the approximately 58 million students in public school, public schools teach nearly 29 times the number of students as are in the homeschool environment.

Also, those students in the homeschool environment have a one (or more) on one learning environment while in public school they have a 29, or more, to one student to teacher environment. As a result, public schools must attend to the "mean" needs of the community's students. This attention often leaves gaps in the needs of the individual students. These gaps need not exist in a homeschool environment.

After our little digression, let's return to our gifted or talented student. When we decide to homeschool, it is important we screen the child for her capabilities, background, interests, and current levels of knowledge and understanding. In our case with our grandson, we used an interview process and sat through several discussions with his middle school counselor.

A parent often knows through teacher conferences and other interactions with school administration and merely observing and interacting with the student what circumstances drove the parent into a homeschooling decision. The earlier that decision is made the better. Often, the parent is dissatisfied with the learning environment she sees on the school campus. Safety considerations and her son or daughter's behavior have become driving issues.

The interested homeschool parent should understand the usefulness of student grades. Often a parent sees good grades and assumes that their daughter or son is an academic whiz, or that behavioral issues spell out a substandard student. Neither of these may be correct.

As is often the case, surprises are in store. Our grandson was in classes for special or under-performing students, on one of the many programs offered that provide a higher level of state support for needy families. We interviewed him in-depth and determined that all was not as it appeared to be. He had no obvious behavioral problems outside the factor that he found it difficult to cope with established boundaries since he had had none and his grades were far below the averages of the non-program students.

With the approval of his mother, and with the support and direction of his guidance counselor, we got him off his special program and took him for homeschooling. As we were testing his capabilities, we found that although he was in the ninth-grade, his reading was below a second-grade level! To counter this, his reading and English skills became our first priority, knowing that his studies in other subjects would also be positively impacted. He developed his skills in reading and was eventually at grade level. This was important as when Scott returned to regular classes, no longer identified as a special needs student, he made honor roll and became, in his own eyes, successful. In other words, Scott was actually a bright student that had been pigeonholed in a special state-sponsored program. There are many like Scott.

According to Glenna Kuhlman,[7] 'The abilities of many bright or gifted children are not recognized by the classroom teacher, because they may seem unattached to the topic at hand. They might not be the A students or even the most engaged student who often has his hand up to answer questions. Some students who are bright may not act "appropriately". The "A" student and the student that acts "appropriately" are NOT necessarily gifted. The bright and/or gifted student may be fidgety, may tend to be distracted, or due to boredom, may even be troublemaker in an attempt to not be labeled a "nerd".'

'Bright students do not often get the challenges other students do in the standard curriculum; they need more. With minds starved for information and activity, that energy may find other, often dysfunctional, avenues in which to manifest itself. Homeschooling can add dimension to the bright student's education.' It is frequently the case that these children seek greater attention, and when they do not receive it may act out for more.

'As a result of the factors mentioned above, some bright or gifted students may be considered as ADHD, Attention Deficit Hyperactivity Disorder. My observation seems to indicate that although ADHD is often a label assigned to a student by a school counselor, teacher, or administrator, such labels tend to stick and follow a child. Labeling is easy and the malady can account for many unwanted behaviors. The parent is told that his child is ADHD should, if possible, get a second diagnostic opinion from a competent psychologist or psychiatric professional. **Non-drug** therapy may be appropriate. In some cases, but not all, drug therapy may be recommended. Before accepting this treatment for your child, I suggest you research information on the drug's side effects.'

---

[7] Interview with Glenna M. Kuhlman, August 2017, Presidential Award in Teaching Elementary Mathematics, Contributor to the New Jersey Mathematics Standards; recognized expert in teaching the gifted and Talented Student.

To counter the various issues that may be present, the homeschool parent must provide challenges that the public schools may not. A good resource for finding out what materials are available and how to use them is Dr. Madeline Hunter. [8]There are many other materials and resources available, some free and some at a reasonable cost. You may also try

http://www.nagc.org/resourcespublications/resources/my child-gifted/common-characteristics-giftedindividuals/traits. In addition to material, the time involved must increase as well. The brighter students need more challenges over longer time durations to keep their interest.

The opposite end of the spectrum is the special needs child. Special needs cover a lot of territory and can be anything from a misapplied label, as our grandson was, to autism, Down's syndrome, or other physical, emotional, or psychological disorder. Unless there is an obvious determining factor, professional help should be sought for the resources to meet those students' unique needs. To provide an appropriate learning environment for these children, specialized equipment may be necessary such as readers for vision-impaired children to amplified equipment for the hearing-impaired.

As we saw with our grandson's circumstance, labels are often inappropriately applied. Once labeled, the state system is geared to keeping the child in the system. Sometimes because it means more money will be granted, sometimes because well-meaning educators believe it is the best "thing" for the child, and other times because that decision has been just carried over from year to year.

As you will note in the assessment chapter, all educational organizations should be appropriately audited, both internally and externally. Such evaluations are sometimes not

---

[8] Dr. Madeline Hunter, The Madeline Hunter Model of Mastery Learning

performed as needed because of the expense and budgetary problems in a district. This is important to the homeschool parent as it identifies a matter with which she may find it necessary to handle. Our grandson seemed stuck in the latter category. It took Glenna and me, two professional educators, to change his status.

When I was young and living in Buffalo, New York, my best friend Gary had to go to the hospital in the middle of the night. It was determined that he had acute hemophilia and could no longer attend public school. Eventually, all his schooling was done at home. Although we remained close friends, I was told I could only visit if I was very careful around him. If Gary took a step on his own feet, his feet would be badly bruised. A simple scratch was a desperate situation as he immediately began to bleed, and stopping bleeding could only be done in the hospital.

Gary made a good student and was a good friend, but his world became a padded existence in which his every move had to be monitored. This was difficult for his parents, but it had to be done. My place in this story was to provide a "normal" friend relationship for him, an important psychological resource. As a young boy, to me, this was merely a nice place and person to visit. I would find out years later, after his passing away, that it was very important to Gary. Special needs students may need extensive support in their own learning environment, which may extend further into the community.

Whether your special needs child is like either Scott or Gary, you must determine that child's needs and provide a suitable place that meets the requirements those needs or unique circumstances generate. By unique, we mean factors that affect the child that are specific to that child in the human circle in which he lives his life. A behavioral issue, perhaps due to a hormonal imbalance, may be relatively common to a doctor, but within the family and daily human interactions, the child's needs may seem complex, quizzical, and "unique".

<u>Self-Assessment Questionnaire</u>

Did you read the entire chapter? Yes ☐ No ☐

List three things you got out of the chapter:

1.

2.

3.

How will you apply these things to teaching your student?

Congratulations on completing this chapter!

Chapter 3
Goals and Objectives

As in everything we do, we must have goals identified. Goals should be written down and kept available for use in our decision-making system. When we make a decision, we must first ask, "Will this get me closer to my goal?"

Goals are written at three levels; experts identify these as primary, secondary, and tertiary. Some professionals use first, second, and third; yet others refer to long-term, short-term, and immediate. The difference is typically in the environment used, academics, engineering, business, etc. Whichever labels you chose, stay consistent with them. No matter what you call them, take the time to understand it and do it. A rule of thumb is, "If they aren't written down, they aren't done."

Businesses spend large sums for goals training and take great pains to build entire planning structures around them. These goals are used in making every business-related decision so that the business can stay on track and attain the stated goal. You should take goal setting as seriously and use the goals in the same way business does. Engineers use goals in much the same way so that they can complete their projects on time and under budget.

In goal setting, we have two parts. The first is the establishment of the goals. The second is the establishment of objectives used to attain them. A goal has an achievable end to a process that is difficult, but not impossible, to attain. Objectives are the steps that are necessary to make in order to meet your goals. These will vary depending on the needs of your student.

Let's look at goal setting, "What is the first thing often thought of in the school process?"

You are right! Grades.

What grades are we most concerned with?

When we consider growth in academics, we consider going to college among the most important goals...but college is not the only option. To get to college, two tests are generally required. The first is the Scholastic Aptitude Test (SAT) and the next, an Achievement Test (ACT); there may be two or more ACTs required for a particular school, such as language or mathematics. These are usually written at the high school level. Many colleges and universities require an autobiography or a writing sample to show the student's ability to use written language.

The student must establish his goals, although a parent, guardian, or caregiver may provide guidance. It is essential that the student has "bought into the idea". When your student establishes his goals, he must be pragmatic in his perspective. He may not want to go through the collegial process. He may wish to join the workforce or enter the military first. Entering the military is a positive way to help pay for a college education.

Scaffolding
A good tool when developing and using goals is scaffolding. In scaffolding, the parent and student determine

the relevancy of their established goals. [9]Scaffolding is a teaching strategy to stimulate a 'child's interest in the task, establishing and maintaining an orientation towards task-relevant goals, highlighting critical features of the task that the child might overlook, demonstrating how to achieve goals, and help to control frustration.'

(Wood & Wood, 1996, p. 5) The teacher helps the student master a task or concept that the student is initially unable to grasp independently. The teacher offers assistance with only those skills that are beyond the student's capability. Of great importance is allowing the student to complete as much of the task as possible, unassisted.

Grandson Scott wanted to work as a power company wireman on the high towers. This was his primary goal. To accomplish this, he needed to achieve several secondary goals. One was to get an Associate Degree in Electrical Engineering from a local community college. Another way was to pass a pole-climbing test. The third was to succeed in passing a multi-level interview process. Each of these secondary goals had third-level or tertiary goals that had to be met. In meeting his goals, he identified the steps he had to take to attain the goals. These steps were his objectives. As he completed his objectives, he got closer and closer to his goal. He is now doing what he wants to do as an electrical journeyman.

[9] Wood, D., & Wood, H. (1996). Vygotsky, Tutoring and Learning. *Oxford Review of Education, 22*(1), 5–16.

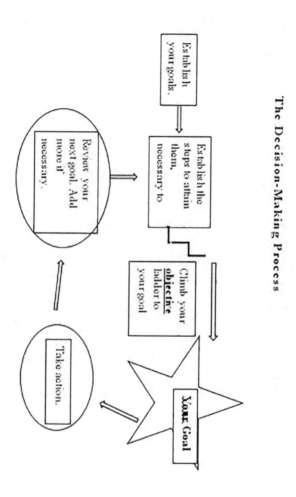

The Decision-Making Process

If you haven't established goals and objectives, let me help walk you through it by giving you a few hints. First, I recommend an outline format. Establish a list of goals.

i. Interview my student (primary).
ii. Establish a relationship with an accredited organization (secondary).

iii. Determine the curriculum (secondary).
iv. Get my student to buy into the program (primary).
v. Identify a learning space (tertiary).
vi. Organize necessary materials (tertiary).
vii. Begin classes (primary).
viii. Complete the grade level (secondary).
ix. Take the SAT (primary).
x. Take the ACTs (primary).

Once you have identified your goals, enter the steps you believe are necessary to attain them. Please note that these lists are merely examples, and your list will vary substantially if not entirely.

I. Interview my student (primary).
    1. Student completes questionnaire.
    2. Personal interview with student.
    3. Student writes down her ideas and preferences.

These are your goals

II. Establish a relationship with an accredited organization (secondary).
    1. Contact neighborhood school.
    2. Contact test service.
    3. Contact 2 commercial homeschool contractors.
    4. Identify potential tutors for topical studies.
    5. Parent self-training.

These are your objectives

III. Determine the curriculum (secondary).
IV. Get my student to buy into the program (primary)
    1. Have student establish study rules.
    2. Have student sign or initial the rules.
V. Identify a learning space (tertiary).

VI.   Organize necessary materials (tertiary).
VII.   <u>Begin Classes (primary).</u>
VIII. Complete the grade level (secondary).
IX.   <u>Take the SAT (primary).</u>
X.   <u>Take the ACTs (primary).</u>

Fill in the remainder to meet the needs you have identified. Interestingly, once you have begun to write down your ideas objectives can easily become goals requiring additional objectives.

[10]*Tulane University, Tips for Writing Goals and Objectives, www.tulane.edu*
A common way of describing goals and objectives follows:

- *A goal is an overarching principle that guides decision making while objectives are specific, measurable steps that can be taken to meet the goal.*
- *Goals are broad while objectives are narrow.*
- *Goals are general intentions while objectives are precise.*
- *Goals are intangible while objectives are tangible.*
- *Goals are abstract while objectives are concrete.*
- *Goals are generally difficult to measure while objectives are measurable.*

As a homeschool parent, you must understand that you are only one-half of the equation. The second half is your student. It is more than desirable to get your student on board. You must incorporate his/her perceived needs and desires as well…as long as they help attain the desired goals. You may want to incorporate her ideas into defining goal objectives.

---

[10] Tulane University, Tips for Writing Goals and Objectives, www.tulane.edu

Self-Assessment Questionnaire

Did you read the entire chapter? Yes ☐   No ☐

List three things you got out of the chapter:
1.

2.

3.

How will you apply these things to teaching your student?

Congratulations on completing this chapter!

Chapter 4
Communication, the Foundation of Method

Communication is essential. By communication, we consider all material to be taught presented using two or more methods in a manner that will ensure, as best as possible, full understanding between the student and the parent. We submit several qualifiers: the student's mental or  emotional ability restrictions for skill level; whether or not, the student is physically able to understand, and the ability and willingness for student and parent to relate to each other positively.

We know that people learn by different means. Students learn auditorily, visually, and kinesthetically, or emotionally.[11] Eric Combs, Dr. Aaron Dahlgren, and Dr. Diane I.M. Wittig in their book, Time To Teach, Differentiated Instruction: Engagement and Motivation in Every Classroom, stated:

What are the modalities of learning?

Four of the primary receiving modalities for learning are auditory, visual, kinesthetic, or emotional. The quality of

[11] Eric Combs, Dr. Aaron Dahlgren, and Dr. Diane I.M. Wittig, Time To Teach, Differentiated Instruction: Engagement and Motivation in Every Classroom, May 2014, Hayden Lake, ID, Center For Teacher Effectiveness. (page 6)

receptivity for learning comes from the match between how the student receives the information and how the student best learns.

It is the challenge for the parent to use at least two of these methods in their communication with her student. With developed skill, the parent may be able to combine all four modalities.

Most of us understand what these modalities refer to. Auditory is hearing; Visual is eyesight, and kinesthesis is touch. But how can we incorporate emotional modality? In employing an emotional modality, since emotions in the student is most easily triggered through his experience and learned perceptions, you can use descriptions of personal experiences and other forms of anecdotal information. Many demonstration techniques can exude an emotional response as well.

The parent must be aware that eliciting an emotional response has both positive and negative potential. A child or youth can easily be worked up, aggravated, or get incorrect impressions that may be long lasting and have a negative result. Stay positive!

When most of us perceive of communication during the teaching process, we often think of a teacher in front of the classroom. This perception was at one time true, and movies, articles, joke cards, and a multitude of media venues have supported this view. Instead, communicating in teaching is a very complex issue that takes into consideration gender, demographics, cultures, and individual learning capabilities and skills. The homeschool parent will be surprised at this complexity once he begins to teach his own son or daughter and finds out that the person they have been living with, supporting, and thought they knew is probably quite different and multifaceted.

We can believe all day that we are providing the perfect responses to our students learning needs. Maybe, but the first thing that the homeschool parent must learn is that without effective communication, learning will NOT happen. Good communication takes place using several modalities, not merely vocal. It includes the use of aides, sound, and touch. Learning modalities can also include temperature and scent. In fact, since the communication level we are seeking is intended to generate an emotional response of some type, we find it best to incorporate several mutually supporting modalities to increase the student's internalization of the material being taught.

Let's begin with the basics we might consider as traditional communication skills.

[12]According to Toastmaster International
Begin with five points:
- Know your subject.
  Be competent in your subject. Prepare your presentation and if you do not know, look up the essential information and use other resources. Students do not expect their teachers to be perfect; they expect them to be prepared.
- Know your audience and your space.
  Whether you are homeschooling a single student or speaking before a large audience, you must know that audience. This knowledge includes both the student's external features such as gender, physical capabilities, and size. The homeschool parent must also be aware of the student's internal features such as gender or gender preferences and keys to enable the student's learning.
- Never apologize.

---

[12] Taken from, Toastmaster International, Five Speaking Points, https://www.toastmasters.org/Find-a-Club/05282335-talkingpoints

The prepared teacher can make errors; this is just a matter of being human. However, it is essential that the student has trust in her teacher or parent as a teacher. Indicating an error is not the same as submitting an apology, as an apology indicates a fault rather than an error.

- Imagine yourself giving a great speech. An important part of teaching is the acceptance of the teacher's own capabilities. Before opening a book or meeting her student, the teacher, [parent or professional, must know that she is going to do a great job].
- Focus on your message, not yourself.
  The teacher must remind himself that the goal is the advancement of the student and the attaining of the student's educational goals.

[13]Four Cornerstones of Public Speaking Are HAIL

- H Honesty
  Be clear in your communication without hidden agendas or half-truths. Understand that the half-truth is the worst kind of lie as it has the ring of honesty.
- A Authenticity
  You are who you are and if you pretend to be otherwise, it will be discovered to the loss of your credibility.
- I Integrity
  If you give a direction for example, live up to it yourself and expect your student to do the same.
- L Love
  Love your student. Praise her successes and sympathize with her pains.

Your student's success is certainly shared by you as well.

---

[13]Taken from, Toastmaster International, HAIL, https://www.toastmasters.org/Find-a-Club/05282335-talkingpoints

There has been a great deal of study done on the best methods to communicate, or present, material to a student. Although much in these methods is very sophisticated and is often considered the realm of the professional educator, the homeschool parent should have enough familiarity with them to help her establish and apply a proper curriculum for her son or daughter, nephew or niece, grandson or granddaughter.

I mentioned that much of these methods were for the benefit of the professional educator. The language of education is one such segregator between the education professional and the homeschool lay instructor. Don't let yourself be cowed by these terms. They are seldom as difficult as written. They are often thoroughly filled with psychobabble and unnecessarily long or coined verbiage. For instance, the term pedagogy (ped-a-gojie) can simply be replaced by the lay teacher as "methods". We will also deal with "taxonomies" or descriptions for methods application. We will discuss in particular Bloom's Taxonomy, which happens to be a long-used model for teaching higher thinking skills, and the [14]Gradual Release of Responsibility (GRR) methods that may better apply to the homeschool environment.

When we study the results of effective communication and teaching methods, the results are fairly consistent globally when you take into consideration of such factors as gender perspectives.

[15]Anderson and Haddad (2005) female students felt more free to voice their opinions in an online environment, and that they perceived a deeper level of learning as a result.

---

[14] Fischer, D., & Frey, N. (2003). Writing instruction for struggling adolescent readers: A gradual release model. *Journal of Adolescent & Adult Literacy, 46*(5), 396–405.

[15] Anderson, D. M., & Haddad, C. J. (2005). Gender, voice, and learning in online course environments. *Journal for Asynchronous Learning Networks. 9*, 3–14.

[16]A females' brain has more connections between the right and left halves.

It has been known for a long time that women tend to excel at language-based learning. Whereas, men have traditionally been considered more skilled at math, science, and spatial reasoning. Women are superior communicators for several reasons. First, they use both halves of their brain for communication, while men typically only use the left side.

[17]Women also have a much more developed limbic system, which puts them more in touch with their feelings. Because of this, women are able to feel connected to others more easily.

[18]Women are more in touch with their feelings, and more adept at communication. Women are [19]more likely to want to discuss problems and issues while men generally deal with problems differently.

While men are competitive in many areas, many women are in constant competition with each other on a more personal level.

Students have expressed their preferences for successful teaching methods. In addition, many surveys and studies have been completed, both domestically and internationally, that indicate the most successful methods. The results indicate that students fare best in a "Blended methodology". A teaching method that is neither fully online nor fully in the classroom, instead it combines teaching means from both. For our needs

---

[16] Jay Patterson (1999). Female Perception vs. Male Perception pg. 1, para. 4

[17] Jay Patterson (1999). Female Perception vs. Male Perception, pg. 1, para.6

[18] Jay Patterson (1999). Female Perception vs. Male Perception, pg. 1, para. 8

[19] Jay Patterson (1999). Female Perception vs. Male Perception

of the successful homeschool parent, we recommend and will consider this teaching format to be the most appropriate. The Blended method incorporates both the benefit of direct interaction with the parent instructor and the use of online resources.

Self-Assessment Questionnaire

Did you read the entire chapter? Yes ☐   No ☐

List three things you got out of the chapter:

1.

2.

3.

How will you apply these things to teaching your student?

Congratulations on completing this chapter!

Chapter 5
The Application of Effective Teaching Methods

In this chapter, we will delve into some new and interesting material for the lay teacher. This is where the homeschool parent meets the technology of teaching.

I was reviewing some articles yesterday about the use of knowledge. I came across the concept of the Gnosis Framework (Gnosis: *Greek*; knowledge based). I had once studied Gnostic Christian concepts, which related to the gathering of knowledge of and about Christ and His church. If we expand this to education, we might equate a Gnostic framework to a large boiling pot of spaghetti in which each strand of the spaghetti is like a piece of knowledge or experience. We can consider the cooking pot as the full content of accumulated knowledge of both the teacher and her student or students.

One failure of Gnostic Christianity was that the amassed knowledge became too great to be useful. It was eventually discredited by formal and specific doctrines. The Gnostic concept can be applied to any content of learning and experience, but a means of withdrawing specific and needed information from the mass is needed. The framework is a means of retrieving information from this boiling moving mass of spaghetti. In our case, our framework is our taxonomies. Our preferred taxonomies are Bloom's Taxonomy, the institution standard, and GRR (Gradual Release of Responsibility).

Bloom's Taxonomy is considered by most educators as the standard for educating children in the use of higher level thinking skills. Since it is considered a standard, we will discuss the taxonomy in some depth as well as its application in the homeschool environment. When reading this, be aware that we are writing through the lens of homeschool education.

There is a multitude of sources of information about Bloom's Taxonomy. Our source for our discussion of Bloom's Taxonomy (Bloom's) is [20]Bloom's Taxonomy, Learning Strategies, or Instructional Strategies, Donald Clark (1999). Bloom's is one of three domains in a matrix of "learning domains". Bloom (1956) defines the "Cognitive Domain". The two other domains are the Affective Domain (Krathwohl, Bloom, & Masia, 1973) and the Psychomotor Domain (Simpson, 1972). We will work primarily within Bloom's Cognitive Domain.

Bloom's Taxonomy divides the Cognitive Domains into six categories. These are, from the most basic to the highest-level thinking skills: Knowledge, Comprehension, Application, Analysis, Synthesis, and Evaluation. We are all human and therefore, we each have talents, capabilities, and limitations. When we teach, our goal is for our students to attain the highest thinking level they can achieve. Not all will reach the most advanced levels, but that is not the problem. The issue is in the attempt and attaining success at your student's greatest potential. For this reason, we strongly prefer formative assessment strategies rather than the more

---

[20] Clark DR (1999), Bloom's Taxonomy, Learning Strategies or Instructional Strategies, retrieved from http://www.nwlink.com/hrd/strategy.html

common summative assessment strategies. We will talk more about these in our next chapter.

[21]Description of Bloom's Cognitive Domain Categories:

Knowledge (Learn)
The provision of information through a number of techniques such as lectures, demonstrations, visual and audio aids, observation, and summative question and answer time.

Comprehension (Understand)
We are strong on the Socratic Method, which is the instilling of understanding in the student by question and discussion.

Application (Put the knowledge to work)
Role-playing, surveys, and case studies help in understanding how to apply the learned information.

Analysis (Discover an action's essential components)
Determining value in the application of knowledge. The Socratic Method helps at this learning level. The student learns how to dissect information and reconstruct it to use it effectively.

Synthesis (Construct a solution)
The learner can put together information from his knowledge, whether from his own or researched knowledge, to meet a perceived need. For example, how can we plan for an event such as a disaster? We know that one will occur; we do not know what it will be or when and where it will happen.

Evaluation (Determine the value of a possible solution)

---

[21] Clark DR (1999), Bloom's Taxonomy, Learning Strategies or Instructional Strategies, retrieved from http://www.nwlink.com/hrd/strategy.html

The learner can identify results from an action, either real or perceived. Based upon his learning, or gleaned knowledge, he can judge, and estimate its value.

There are several formats of learning that you, as a homeschool parent, should be aware. We will talk more about these in a later chapter. The first of concern to you is **Distance Learning (DL)**. In essence, this is learning through online resources and through information gleaned from the internet.

Lecturing

Lecturing is the most traditional of the formats. While excellent in providing information (declarative knowledge), lectures often lack in knowing and understanding how to apply learned knowledge (procedural knowledge).

It is said that, 'A picture is worth a thousand words.' This is true at home as well. The format using **Teaching or Performance Aids** gives credence to that statement. Teaching Aids includes almost any media type, models, flowcharts, maps, music, and the list is infinite. Anything useful in getting knowledge and understanding to your student is an effective Teaching Aid.

Teaching aids have another important secondary purpose. A student and teacher working together in constructing or choosing effective teaching aids help with the socialization of the student as he would be required to work as a team with you and others while finding or creating useful aids.

With your student, think of projects. Hands-on work that includes research and planning can meet all student-learning types and can also be an enjoyable project. Projects are excellent for socialization and the development of higher learning skills.

Utilize **Action learning** in your presentation.

[22]Action learning is a continuous process of learning and reflection with the intention of getting something done. It does not use project work, job rotation, or any form of a simulation such as case studies or business games. Learning is centered around the need to find a solution to a real problem. Most action learning processes take from four to nine months to complete. Learning is voluntary and learner-driven. In addition, individual development is just as important as finding the solution to the problem (Revans, 1998).

Blended Learning

Blended learning is a relatively new teaching method. As you noticed, there are many methods available to the teacher. The question often becomes, "Which shall I use?" Blended learning provides the answer to that question. As the name indicates, blended learning is a composite of a grouping of methods organized to meet your child's needs. You, the homeschool parent, can combine the benefits of online distance learning. Active learning, performance aids, and any group of learning methods into a single means of teaching. The key here is to plan the organization of the methods to meet the desired goals. I consider this the most desirable method for teaching at home.

[23]Ellis, Wagner, & Longmire wrote a set of learner-centered principles for training in 1999 that will serve the homeschool parent in teaching through the active learning process.

---

[22] Revans, R. W. 1998. *ABC of action learning*. London: Lemos and Crane.

[23] Ellis, Wagner, & Longmire, 1999), Managing Web-based training: How to keep your program on track and make it successful, *Set of Learner-centered Principals for Training, Alexandria,* VA: ASTD Press

1. Learning does not occur in a vacuum. Learners discover and construct meaning from information and experience based on their unique perceptions, thoughts, and feelings.
2. More information doesn't necessarily mean more learning. Learners seek to create meaningful uses of knowledge regardless of the quantity and quality of information presented.
3. Learners link new knowledge to existing information in ways that make sense to them. The remembering of new knowledge is facilitated when it can be tied to a learner's current knowledge.
4. Personality influences learning. Learners have varying degrees of self-confidence and differ in the clarity of their personal goals and expectations for success and failure.
5. Learners want to learn. Individuals are naturally curious and enjoy learning but personal insecurity and fear of failure often get in the way.
6. Learners like challenges and are most creative when it is challenging and meets their individual needs.
7. Learners are individuals. Not all learners are at the same stage of physical, intellectual, emotional, and social development. Learners also differ in their cultural backgrounds. Although the basic principles of learning apply to all learners regardless of these differences, trainers must take into account such differences between learners.
8. The learning environment is important. Learners learn best in a friendly, socially interactive, and diverse environment.
9. Learners like positive reinforcement. Learning environments that support the self-esteem and respect of the individual learner tend to be more successful.
10. Past experience matters. Personal beliefs and impressions from prior learning color the learners' worldviews and their approach to learning.

You now have an idea of what Bloom entails and what our teaching goals are. Now how do you get the information and knowledge into the hands of your learner in a positive way? To do this, we will refer to our second taxonomy GRR or [24]Gradual Release of Responsibility.

Gradual Release of Responsibility

What are we releasing in Gradual Release of Responsibility or what are we responsible for? In essence, we are releasing the responsibility of teaching so that gradually more and more the student will become more effective in self-teaching.

Most homeschool parents are not technical experts in multiple disciplines. However, most can be excellent guides to their learners as their learners grow through the educational process.

Why is this true? It is true because the parent, by committing to the homeschool process, has an established personal bond with the student to care that her student succeeds. As that recognized education expert, [25]Madeline Hunter (1984) said: 'Kids don't care how much you know until they know how much you care.' Your student knows you care and therefore, will support your cooperative efforts that will result in their success and betterment. Think of yourself as an enabler rather than an expert.

GRR is divided into three phases. The first phase is "I do", the second is "we do", while the third phase is "you do". In the "I do" phase, you will be responsible for establishing goals, establishing and putting a curriculum into effect, and explaining ideas and concepts necessary to provide the learner with a beginning foundation.

---

[24] Fischer, D., & Frey, N. (2003). Writing instruction for struggling adolescent readers: A gradual release model. *Journal of Adolescent & Adult Literacy, 46*(5), 396–405.

[25] Hunter, Madeline. (1984). Knowing, Teaching, and Supervising.

Your student will begin to grow in her learning once her curriculum foundation is set. Built upon your caring relationship with her, she will want to move forward with you. The concept of "with you" is the driver for entering this "we do" phase. You should notice after reading the information about Bloom that this phase change seems to move the student from Bloom's *Knowledge* category to *Comprehension*. In this phase, new information is learned and organized, ready to be retrieved when needed[26] (Groundwater-Smith et al., 1998).

In this "we do" phase, the student learns much. He learns about learning cooperatively. When help is needed, he begins to grasp self-sufficiency in learning and begins to gain confidence by understanding his capabilities and limitations. He will move ahead into Bloom's higher learning skill levels.

As a student gains confidence and begins to recognize her capabilities and limitations, she will begin to function on her own. This desire for self-sufficiency in her learning process is her entry into the third phase of GRR or the "you do" phase. This transition from one phase to the next and finally into the last is the gradual release of your responsibility for her training to her responsibility for her learning.

With a group of students, this phase can be separated by "you" plural or "you" singular. As a homeschool parent, the "you" for you is usually singular. This phase is student-centered learning rather than parent-centered teaching.

In this phase, you, the parent, becomes a facilitator. Although you may need to obtain a tutor for presenting some technical information or to make up for the information you do not know, your responsibility is to enable your student to research and apply information for themselves. Referring back to Bloom, once to achieve this phase, you are entering into the student learning and grasping the highest levels of

---

[26] Groundwater-Smith, S., Le Cornu, R. J., & Ewing, R. A. (1998). *Teaching: challenges and dilemmas*: Harcourt Brace.

learning they are able to do. You will have met at least one primary goal.

Self-Assessment Questionnaire

Did you read the entire chapter? Yes ☐ No ☐

List three things you got out of the chapter:

1.

2.

3.

How will you apply these things to teaching your student?

Congratulations on completing this chapter!

Chapter 6
Assessment: Your Student, Your Program, and You

Like businesses everywhere that use internal and external audits to ensure proper functioning of their businesses, you should do the same, whether a homeschool parent or an interested parent with a public-school

100%

student. Most important, however, is your own student's learning.

Effective assessment of your learner's educational growth is essential. Assessment is not the same as grading. Grading is a small part of assessment but necessary for college, administrative, and statutory consideration.

Assumption Number One: We All Seek Success

Success can be defined in many ways depending on the environment, individual or community perspective, history or personal background, and the comparisons that success will be likened to. Dictionary definitions may not be as complete or specific as needed for defining success for an individual student or parent. Defining success is complex, similar to establishing what "is" is.

As a homeschool parent, you also need to define what success will be for your student. In this definition, you must take a number of things into consideration. The more factors you can identify the more accurate your definition will be. Be aware that too many factors will begin to make your definition too burdensome for meaningful application. In most cases, the "as the teacher may direct" option is included to meet changing or unexpected factors.

Assumption Number Two: Success Must Be Measurable

How do you measure something as potentially nebulous as success? We do this by establishing an assessment procedure, writing the procedure down, obtaining a "buy-in" by those being assessed, and applying that procedure consistently.

There are two types of assessment of interest to us; one is <u>summative</u> and the other is formative. Summative assessment is what most of us consider grading. It is purely objective and represents only what a student earns on papers, projects, and tests.

As stated, assessment typically takes two forms, "formative" and "summative". When considering the term "summative", consider the root word "sum" which is a mathematical expression indicating the objective nature of the term. Look at summative assessment as being fact-based. When considering the term "formative", consider its root word "form", which is indicative of a subjective evaluation for correctness, applicability, and consistency rather than merely a correct answer without adequate understanding that is sometimes found under strict summative assessments. Consider formative assessment as being demonstrably understanding and applicability based.

Use the summative assessment method to measure the level of short-term topical proficiency. Summative assessment provides a grade point or letter result. This form of assessment gives a student a grade that places her among comparisons with other students. Summative assessment is useful for administrations to prove their effectiveness for funding, meeting state-mandated testing requirements, school assessment, or program placement. The unfortunate issue is that none of these truly represents the student's grasp of a subject in the higher thinking skills.

Teachers today subscribe to the use of both forms but tend to perceive one or the other as being most applicable. Most teachers and their districts, states, and national labor organizations perceive the summative approach very useful. The summative grade structure, either numeric (%) or alphabetic (A-F) in its simplicity, is in the idea that if a student gets his or her facts straight, he or she knows the subject well enough, and the facts can be counted. You can see this in the systemic reliance on tests that include multiple choices, true-false, fill-in-the-blanks, best answer, and right or wrong answer. These are easily tallied.

Both summative and formative assessments make use of essay questions. These questions cross the boundaries of both types of assessment and sometimes tint the summative approach with colors from the formative method. You will notice that the essay approach is much less used. It is burdensome for the grader and requires a greater and specific understanding of the subject by the assessor. The assessor must be able to understand and make a value judgment of the implication of the student's intended response.

There are some advantages for the student in summative assessment. It provides the student with an immediate feedback. For that reason, it can be motivational as the student attempts to reach a successful attainment of her learning goals. Teachers find quick assessment and comparisons between their students without the additional work required in formative assessment methods.

[27] Summative (High-Stakes) Assessments:

Summative assessment techniques evaluate student learning. These are high-stakes assessments (i.e., they have high point values) that occur at the end of an instructional unit or course. They measure the extent to which students have achieved the desired learning outcomes.

Use formative assessment to guide growth and development in student learning. Formative assessment is more difficult to control due to its many subjective facets.

Formative assessment incorporates some quizzes to ensure a factual understanding but relies more on teachers/student oral interviews, observation, subject discussions, table-top drills (a form of desk-top training where a student or study team tests their knowledge, methods, and concepts), and such methods as "Fishbowls" and small-group breakouts. An extreme formative approach assumes a certain level of knowledge by the student. For this reason, the formative approach is most often found in the higher grades, or once the survey courses are taken.

Any delay in introducing the student to the formative assessment method while waiting for the student to apply higher-level thinking skills seems unfortunate because the student would not have had an opportunity to develop formative methods in building his or her learning skills foundation. Educational institutions, under both social and traditional pressures, hold closely to 'school year' calendars. These do not often allow adequate time for formative assessment methods while attempting to meet extensive summative testing mandates by local, state, and federal bureaucracies.

---

[27] University of Texas at Austin, Faculty Innovation Center © 2016–2017

A good home-school program or a more student-valued public-school structure with fewer mandates can resolve this issue by incorporating more formative methods into the student's education in the home. Students learn at differing paces, and their topical growth varies as they develop in maturity, world-knowledge, and ability to understand and assess concepts for themselves.

[28] Formative (Low-Stakes) Assessments:

Formative assessment techniques monitor student learning during the learning process. The feedback gathered is used to identify areas where students are struggling so that instructors can adjust their teaching and students can adjust their studying. These are low-stakes assessments, which should happen early and often in the semester.

Notice that at the end of each chapter, I have provided a few questions. These questions not only provide an opportunity for you to assess yourself and guide you into completing the book but also reinforces the information provided in the text so that you can internalize and mentally organize the material so that you can recall it on demand.

[29] According to Harlen and James (1997), formative assessment:

- Is essentially positive in intent. In that, it is directed towards promoting learning. It is, therefore, part of teaching.

---

[28] University of Texas at Austin, Faculty Innovation Center © 2016–2017

[29] Harlen, W. and James, M., (1997), Assessment and Learning: Differences and Relationships between Formative and Summative Assessment, Assessment in Education: Principles, Policy & Practice, 4(3): pp. 365–379.

- It takes into account the progress of each individual, the effort put in and other aspects of learning, which may be unspecified in the curriculum. In other words, it is not purely criterion-referenced.
- It has to take into account several instances in which certain skills and ideas are used and there will be inconsistencies as well as patterns in behavior. Such inconsistencies would be an "error" in a summative evaluation. But in a formative evaluation, they provide diagnostic information.
- Validity and usefulness are paramount in formative assessment and should take precedence over concerns for reliability.
- Even more than assessment for other purposes, formative assessment requires that pupils have a central part in it. Pupils have to be active in their own learning (teachers cannot learn for them) and unless they come to understand their strengths and weaknesses, and how they might deal with them, they will not make progress.

You may ask, "What are some formative methods and why should I use them?" We have spent a lot of time on the assessments. Let's talk about the whys.

Why teach ninth Grade American History to a student in the fifth grade? Why teach Art to a student who does not have the maturity to understand the benefits of art or his or her place with it? This is the same for all subject areas and perhaps more so in the technical disciplines of science and math. The unfortunate answer is too often, 'Because that's the way it's done.' Alternatively, 'We always do it that way.' Again, a good home-school structure can compensate for this if you, the parent, understand assessment structures. The goal is to attain topical success by the time your student is ready for higher-level studies or entry into an adult functioning world.

Whichever methodology you choose to follow, be consistent. Get a buy-in from your student. A buy-in could be a contract as is used in some classrooms and districts. It could be a signature on a copy of a course syllabus or even taking a course once a syllabus is read. In lower grades, depending upon your relationship with your student, the buy-in might be a simple discussion about what is expected and a promise to follow the course direction. This is one reason why we should include the student in the rule-making process.

Assumption number three: Both means of assessment will most probably be necessary for an exact measure of success.

It is important to know that both summative and formative assessment methods be used together in order to establish an accurate picture of a student's knowledge and higher-level thinking skills. As mentioned, formative assessment is much more complex than summative assessment, which is a simple representation of responses being objectively evaluated. [30]K. Lambert of OCPS Curriculum Services (4/2012) has published on the Internet a well-constructed tool of 60 means to be used for formative assessment. Many of the means are specifically for the public-school classroom; however, several are useful to the home-school parents. In an effort to assist parents, I have listed below a number of the ideas from that tally.

Compiled by K Lambert, OCPS Curriculum Services, 4/2012
1. Index Card Summaries / Questions
    Periodically, distribute index cards and ask students to write on both sides, with these instructions: (Side 1) Based on our study of (unit topic), list a big idea that you understand and word it as a summary statement. (Side 2) Identify something about (unit topic) that you do not yet fully understand and word it as a statement or question.

---

[30] K. Lambert of OCPS Curriculum Services (4/2012)

2. One Minute Essay

   A one-minute essay question (or one-minute question) is a focused question with a specific goal that can, in fact, be answered within a minute or two.

3. Student Conference

   One-on-one conversation with your student to check his level of understanding.

4. Self-Assessment

   A process in which students collect information about their own learning, analyze what it reveals about their progress toward the intended learning goals, and plan the next steps in their learning.

5. Quiz

   Quizzes assess your student for factual information, concepts, and discrete skill.

6. Journal Entry

   Student records in a journal her understanding of the topic, concept, or lesson taught. The parent reviews the entry to see if the student has gained an understanding of the topic, lesson, or concept that was taught.

7. Debriefing

   A form of reflection immediately following an activity.

8. Idea Spinner

   The teacher creates a spinner marked into four quadrants and labeled "Predict, Explain, Summarize, Evaluate". After the new material is presented, the parent spins the spinner and asks her student to answer a question based on the location of the spinner.

9. Reader's Theater

   From an assigned text, the student will create a script and perform it.

10. Oral Questioning

How is _____ similar to / different from

_____?

What are the characteristics/parts of
_____?

In what other ways might we show show/illustrate
_____?

What is the big idea, key concept, moral in
_____?

How does _____ relate to
_____?

What ideas/details can you add to
_____?

Give an example of

_____?

What is wrong with

_____?

What might you infer from

_____?

What conclusions might be drawn from

_____?

What question are we trying to answer

_____?

What problem are we trying to solve

_____?

What are you assuming about

_____?

What might happen if

_____?

What criteria would you use to judge/evaluate
_____?

What evidence supports

_____?

How might we prove/confirm

_____?

How might this be viewed from the perspective of

_____?

What alternatives should be considered

_____?

What approach/strategy could you use to

_____?

11. Student Data Notebooks
    A tool for your student to track his learning: Where am I going? Where am I now? How will I get there (to whatever goal has been chosen)?
12. Socratic Seminar
    Student and parent ask questions of one another about an essential question, topic, or selected text. The questions initiate a conversation that continues with a series of responses and additional questions.
13. Newspaper Headline
    Create a newspaper headline that may have been written on the topic we are studying. Capture the main idea of the event.

My wife and colleague is a Presidential Award winner for Excellence in Teaching Elementary Mathematics, with 37 years of experience in front of the classroom. She had attained a level far beyond the strict use of summative assessment alone, as might have been typically expected from a mathematics teacher.

Years of experience and her own achievements in establishing successful educational programs led her to her analysis and application of many types of formative assessment techniques. Not the least of these achievements was the establishment of an exceptional gifted/talented student program, participation in the New Jersey "SITE" program, which is a student invention program that resulted in her students sometimes qualifying for patents, and an annual guiding consortium of schools throughout the county that included representatives from all districts.

These programs and projects led to establishing an effective means of student assessment, which relied heavily on multiple types of formative assessment. Necessarily, but minimally, summative methodologies were incorporated as well: summative, in the context of providing a baseline knowledge of facts, and formative in providing the higher-level thinking skills of analysis, synthesis, and application ([31]Bloom's Taxonomy, Benjamin Bloom, 1949).

I write curriculum for and teach for a Master's Degree program in Disaster and Emergency Management at Nova Southeastern University's College of Medicine. Having taught in public and private educational institutions and industry, in foreign countries in Asia, India, Africa, Middle East, and South America at all grade levels including adult students with various ethnic and religious backgrounds, I have accepted a perspective, what I refer to as a "global perspective" that leans heavily towards formative methods.

My formative method relies on the comprehensive use of visual and tactile techniques as well as the more common auditory method with objective testing (I have found that such testing in itself was inadvertently biased by the assumption that all students respond in the same way, with the same understanding, to all testing types and formats. This is untrue; therefore, the formative method as a means of assessment may be the more important method). I used books, pictures, demonstration, vignettes, student groups and involvement, student assistance, self-discovery, and ethnic research

---

[31] Bloom's Taxonomy, Benjamin Bloom, 1949

sources. I do use quizzes but only to ensure that students understand foundational facts.

I usually use a pass/no-pass assessment process on objective fact-oriented quizzes. Although individuals' abilities for learning vary, the idea that a student did not understand a necessary fact requires an adjustment in the presentation of material. My mastery assessments are primarily carried out through essays to question requiring application (apply, build, choose, construct, develop,), analysis (analyze, categorize, classify, compare, contrast), synthesis (choose, combine, compile, compose, construct, create), and evaluation (conclude, criticize, decide, defend, determine) followed by an in-depth topical interview. The difficult issue is not determining whether or not the student "passed" or not but how to convert a discussion into a summative grade.

To accomplish this:

1.) I have a list of essential concepts and ideas that I expect to be incorporated in the essay and the topical interview.
2.) The student is expected to provide a short and precise written answer to the question. Requiring answers as short a possible also requires the student to determine through analysis what is most important.
3.) Less important content is synthesized into the ensuing interview process.
4.) The student is then asked to provide a self-evaluation and an evaluation of the topical presentation. By counting the points covered by the student in comparison to the expected list provides enough information to extrapolate a summative grade.
5.) The student gets special verbal recognition for additional ideas he/she has identified. Thus, motivation to succeed is increased due to increased self-worth versus an unnecessary tangible reward.

Student Factors and Assessment:

Your student has his or her own preferences, capabilities, and personal goals that may differ from yours. Although they may be fairly close to yours, in their personal goal synthesis, your student's goals will in all likelihood reflect her judgment of your success in attaining your goals. This is normal modeling by you and should be expected.

There is another level of concerns we must consider as well. These are social and ethnic backgrounds, pressures, regional perspectives, and accepted rules. Although public schools, by the fact that they must draw their student bodies from the broader community, you need to be primarily concerned with only your student or students.

The Assessment Process:

Establish a timeline from your stated goals and objectives.

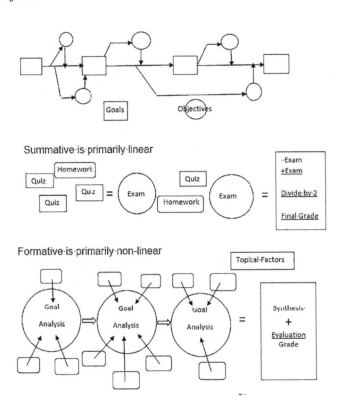

Summative is primarily linear

Formative is primarily non-linear

Since we have made a distinction between the differing concerns of the public-school system and you, why would you need to pay attention to these factors? The simple answer is that as your student, or students in a larger family, gains in his or her appreciation of the broader world, coping and socialization skills must be learned so that your student can take his or her place in the world.

Your student's understanding that as an individual, he/she also has a place in the world community. In 16th century

London, a person generally lived and raised a family in the filth of a relatively small area, often just a few city blocks or as far as the village green. As a 21st century American, however, a student must learn to cope with a worldwide community.

Your student will reflect his private background. I am sure that in the quiet of the night, your student has considered such things as sex and romance; mortality – his own, yours, and the consistency of death; religion, again his own as it relates to yours; travel both locally and internationally and the specifics of right, wrong, good, and evil. Many of these things will come out during his education. You will find that more and more, he will follow his own heart. This is also a natural thing. As you teach, guide your student and enable him to find his own direction. For it is certain that he will find it necessary to use what he has learned. Avoid being critical if his choices are somewhat different than yours. As long as those choices are within accepted law and social constructs under which we all labor, your teaching has had successes.

<u>Self-Assessment Questionnaire</u>

Did you read the entire chapter? Yes ☐   No ☐

List three things you got out of the chapter:

1.

2.

3.

How will you apply these things to teaching your student?

Congratulations on completing this chapter!

Chapter 7
Resources Useful in the Homeschool

Many times parents interested in homeschooling have told me that they did not know where to begin and that they didn't "know enough". Getting into something that has typically been done by  well-trained and licensed professionals, knowing that you do not know as much about different subjects as the team of pros teaching your son or daughter, can be very intimidating. However, statistics indicate that your caring support and guiding presence along with judiciously chosen resources are the measures of success. The two areas provided by you, caring and guidance, can be done no better than you.

Once you decide to homeschool, you must begin establishing an effective home-school environment. This activity includes the provision of good teaching and study places, creating a meaningful schedule that meets the goals you developed in Chapter 3, choosing an appropriate curriculum, finding learning materials, and finding teaching materials. If you are teaching to your student's graduation and she intends to go to college, you must also identify a testing resource.

Things to Do

- Find a place as free of interruptions and outside noises as you are able. Remember, your student will NEED to get adequate sleep, and MUST have a comfortable and clean place as a personal area.

[32]WHY do we need sleep?

Sleep is important for a number of reasons. It restores our energy, fights off illness and fatigue by strengthening our immune system, helps us think more clearly and creatively, strengthens memory, and produces a more positive mood and better performance throughout the day. Sleep isn't just a passive activity and something to fill the time when we are inactive, but rather it is an active and dynamic process vital for normal motor and cognitive function.

HOW MUCH sleep do we need?

Most adults need somewhere between 6–10 hours of sleep per night. Different people need a different amount of sleep to feel rested. If you are frequently tired or irritable during the day and find yourself sleeping more than an extra 2 hours per night on weekends, then you are probably not getting enough sleep during the week. Try for 7–8 hours and see how you feel.

CONSEQUENCES of sleep loss

Lack of sleep is associated with both physical and emotional health risks. These include:

- More illness, such as colds and flu, due to a lowered immune system
- Feeling more stressed out
- Increased weight gain and obesity

---

[32] Taken from https://www.uhs.uga.edu/sleep, University of Georgia, University Health Center

- Lower GPA and decreased academic performance
- Increased mental health issues, such as depression and anxiety
- Increased automobile accidents due to fatigue caused by "drowsy driving"
- Decreased performance in athletics and other activities that require coordination
- A proper amount of sleep is essential for the health and success of your student. Other sites available to refer to include:
- http://kidshealth.org/en/teens/how-much-sleep.html
- https://sleepfoundation.org/sleep-topics/children-and-sleep/page/0/2
- http://www.nationwidechildrens.org/sleep-in-adolescents

You will find that much of your student's quiet time will consist of reading in her private space. Our student had his own cabin on our sailboat, Quiet Passage. He used it more often than we expected. In addition, he had quiet time as needed in the lounge. Having been raised with few boundaries prior to homeschooling with us, we expected less need for him to have private space. We were wrong, and we modified our arrangements for it to work well for him. We always respected that space.

- Secure optional places that your student can use as a change of pace, which will help motivate his studying. Our grandson preferred to go to the city library. Others I have known preferred going to bookstores like Barns and Noble that have a comfortable seating place and the ability to draw books off the counter for research.
- There are numerous accredited programs available with a variety of curricula. I recommend that you review those curricula. Chose three

suitable ones. With your student, chose the one that most reflects your student's needs and interests, meets your budgetary needs and will lead to a future of interest to your student. Remember, as we stated earlier, each decision must lead you closer to your goals; if it doesn't, you must either make another choice or update your student's goals and objectives that are necessary to arrive there.

Your options on which plans to use are great. Without getting into plan quality, since that is a decision you want to make, the decision includes whether you want a parochial teaching environment, secular environment, or a public-school environment.

In many States, you can use the community school's curriculum at little extra cost, but you will lose some of your teaching autonomy. Some commercial or private providers depend on discount pricing, while others depend on word of mouth and reputation. Still, other sources deal with gimmicks, pretty things, and convenience. Costs for these can range from very low to as much as $2,000.00/month.

With some sources, the annual cost is paid up front. Others charge on a course-by-course basis, and yet others charge on a month-by-month basis. Most resources have a range of options based on the level of support they provide. I recommend that you carefully consider the need for too many options so that your cost can be better controlled.

- Find a testing resource that is accredited, has reasonable cost, and is convenient. It is this resource that will provide the appropriate testing and scoring for college entrance examinations or mandated testing required in some states.
- Once you have chosen your curriculum, you will know what materials you will need in the

performance of that curriculum. At a minimum, you will need pencils, paper, and a computer (preferably a laptop or tablet that can be traveled with), which can be used for research, and a printer if possible. Take your time to get comfortable and a magnifying glass of some type (cheap ones do not do well). Get 3x5 cards to be used for taking notes, writing presentation notes, and structuring research projects.

- You must secure your books. Books are an interesting problem. There will be textbooks mandated by your curriculum supplier. If you work through your community school, you may get discounts on used books. If you use a commercial curriculum provider, it will be necessary to use their materials. They are usually high-priced and may be only available through them. This precludes using such discount options as Amazon or eBay.

If you haven't purchased textbooks recently, the cost of books can be shocking. When you are choosing your curriculum providers, be sure to consider the cost of required texts. A single textbook may cost well over $100.

[33]Average Cost of College Textbooks

The National Association of College Stores (NACS) says the average college student will spend **$655** on textbooks each year. But with a single textbook easily costing as much as **$300**, that total can easily be much higher. In fact, the College Board puts the annual cost of books and materials at **$1,168**.

Textbooks are the beginning. You will have additional books that can be purchased through discount resources.

---

[33] College Textbook Prices Increasing Faster Than Tuition And… Downloaded from, www.huffingtonpost.com/2013/01/04/college-textbook-prices-increase_n_2409153.html

During our home-school experience, we purchased numerous books between $8.00 and $15.00. Some were required reading. Some were for research purposes, and some were for the interest and often by the request of our student. We also needed to buy several reference guides in mathematics, English language and grammar, and science. These guides typically run from $8.00 – $11.00.

When putting together your homeschool, it is a good thing to have a list of resources handy while obtaining necessary information and entering into the contracts you require. It may sound as though the points you must complete are numerous and overwhelming. However, most of these are one time only if monitored properly or of small interference and cost if well organized. Keep a log of notes and decisions and make sure it is close at hand when decisions are needed. Each of these factors should be considered as objectives, which are en route to your goals. It is best to be observant and take your time.

I have included the following list of websites to help you in your search. I am not expressing any preferences in this list or making any judgments as to their usefulness to you. I am merely trying to provide you with a good start in your research. Other than reviewing these sites, I have not taken any other methods for their qualification.

It would be nearly impossible for me to provide further qualification without knowing if your student needs any special resources, allotted learning space, allotted time, or the curriculum being followed. Many online schools provide some fairly good materials. The Center for Teacher Effectiveness provides parents with some excellent materials for differentiated instruction and student motivation.

Resources can be materials such as books and pamphlets, electronic learning materials, human resources such as tutors, testing services, legal information, and construction materials for training aids. Costs vary greatly, and to increase sales, often exclude necessary components of the learning process.

As you begin to consider homeschooling, you must determine the regulatory aspects involved. Most states pose no regulatory problems, but a few do. Moreover, some provide access to public schools for such studies as art, physical education, and such extra-curricular activities as sports. Open your homeschool library with a good dictionary. As a style guide, I use *Rules for Writers*, Diana Hacker, 2008 by Bedford/St. Martin's, Boston, Mass.

A Few Important Websites

A few websites that provide important regulatory information are:

https://www.hslda.org/docs/nche/Issues/E/Equal_Access
.pdf
https://projects.propublica.org/graphics/homeschool
https://www.hslda.org/laws/default.asp

It is you, the homeschool parent that makes the difference in your child's success. It is you that sets the boundaries. It is you that motivates your child. It is you that keeps your child on the learning path. Most of all, it is you that models the commitment necessary to get the job done.

There are many online homeschool programs. The following are examples:

https://www.nationalhomeschoolacademy.com/
https://www.acellus.com/homeschool-services/index/
http://landing.keystoneschoolonline.com/lp1/sem/ef/pape
rclip_v2.html?utm_source=Microsoft+Bing+Ads&utm_
medium=cpc&utm_campaign=NN_NB+-+Home+-
+BMM&utm_term=&ad_group=Homeschool+Other&le
ad_source_detail=Microsoft+Bing+Ads&keyword_matc
h=&leadsource=sem&vendor=acronym&vendor=acrony
m&s_kwcid=AL!2165!10!15889543639!24949646269&
ef_id=WT7IpQAAAAwDi89G:20170909214511:s

http://www.nationalhomeschool.com/about-us/

Homeschool costs can fluctuate dramatically between one curricular source and another. Costs often increase as the student advances from PreK and Kindergarten to elementary school, middle school, and high school.

Use the following websites for cost comparisons:

http://www.nationalhomeschool.com/homeschooling-cost/
https://www.homeschoolacademy.com/homeschool-tuition-and-plans/payment-and-shipping-procedures/
https://www.homeschoolacademy.com/homeschool-tuition-and-plans/accredited-homeschool-programs/online/middle-school/

Costs can vary from about $100 per month to over $3,000 yearly.

In some States and communities, homeschoolers can save a substantial amount in tuition by using the public school curriculum. We taught our grandson using his local high school curriculum. Scott was considered a special needs student. However, after several conversations with his mother and his high school teachers and counselor, we had him removed him from his IEP. This proved to be a pivotal decision that led to his success. Glenna and I amended his high school curriculum to meet the restrictions of homeschooling and in this case, to be homeschooled on a cruising sailboat. He completed his ninth-grade year in homeschool. When he returned, he was entered in regular classes and afterward, made the honor roll consistently. The cost we incurred related to auxiliary books, materials, and such equipment as a laptop computer and a microscope.

Just as in the "real world", no one can know everything. In most cases, a tutor may prove essential. Tutors can cost anywhere from $20 to about $45 per hour depending upon the topic, background of the tutor, and the tutor's reputation. Although many tutors are seasoned professionals or teaching retirees, there are many good tutors available at local colleges and universities.

The following websites are of tutoring companies:
The Tutor Doctor:
landing/port-st-lucie/#~v6P127

Varsity Tutors:
https://www.varsitytutors.com/en/tutoringflorida?networkbing=o&matchtype=e&bidmatchtype=be&keyword=tutoring&creative=12387798638&device=c&capaignid=31834980&adgroupid=5206908304&query=tutoring&utm_source=bing&utm_medium=cpc&utm_campaign=Florida&utm_term=tutoring&utm_content=Tutors%20Main

Tutor Care:
https://www.care.com/tutoring-programs-p1087-q18888298.html?null&_qs=1

Private Tutors:
We must note here that there are many highly qualified private tutors available locally. Many are current college students, active or retired teachers, or former industry professionals. One of my good friends, who is a private tutor, Alan M., is a retired industrial engineer and is superb in tutoring math and language. He takes his work very seriously and develops close relationships with his students and their parents. Believe me, most of these tutors are underpaid for the work they do. This usually makes them a very cost-effective resource.

The advantages of private_individual tutors include:

- Your contract is with the tutor alone. He/she is responsible only to you, his employer.

- He is usually chosen for a specific disciplinary area such as English Literature or Calculus.
- The tutor is local and understands the environment that your student lives in.
- The tutor is usually very flexible in time and teaching location.

Student Testing Services:
Some curriculum providers have student testing services on contract. These services may be expensive or included. It is important to know that they work for the provider and not you.

Seton Testing Service
http://www.setontesting.com/
Christian Homeschooler
http://www.christianhomeschoolers.com/hs_testing.html

Please note once again that I have included the listing of services not as a preference but chosen from browser lists to act as a starting point for you, the homeschool parent, to begin your search for appropriate support resources. I have used multiple browsers because their algorithms usually include a rated structure based upon usage.

The following are two resources for teaching materials
http://www.discountschoolsupply.com/
https://www.homeschool.com/articles/Back-To
Homeschool-Awards-2017/Default.asp?nothanks=1

<u>Self-Assessment Questionnaire</u>

Did you read the entire chapter? Yes ☐ No ☐

List three things you got out of the chapter:
1.

2.

3.

How will you apply these things to teaching your student?

Congratulations on completing this chapter!

Chapter 8
Syllabus, Lesson Plans, and Content Research:
Constructing a Course of Instruction

Note: This chapter contains examples of both a syllabus and lesson plan from the author's own list of **What are we doing, and how are we getting it done?** *developed curricula. Reflecting differences in the topic, intent, course goals, and objectives, these examples may be used as guides to help in your understanding and writing of syllabi and lesson plans. These examples may vary greatly from others' examples or your own work.*

Depending upon your choice of curriculum provider and the goals and objectives you have listed for your homeschool student, you may choose to include your own curriculum or change one that is provided for you. To accomplish this, you should understand the factors that go into such an effort. This chapter will provide you with foundational information that will ensure that you will be successful. Your student may have special needs or requirements; therefore, look at this chapter as a guide. We will provide you with ideas regarding student needs to be considered in Chapter 11.

This chapter has been placed in this book at this point so that as you review the following chapters, you will have an idea how to incorporate your student's needs into your new or adjusted curriculum. At any rate, understanding how a course is constructed will help you immensely in your presentation of the subject to your student.

In the beginning of this book, you developed your statement of goals and objectives. If you recall, I mentioned that your goals and objectives may change and that they must be written down. With that list on your desk and a blank sheet of paper next to it, you are ready to begin your construction.

The construction of a course must take heed of several factors that work together. First, be aware of how your curriculum fits contextually with the other courses being presented to your student. If you can write your material so that it reflects the other materials while maintaining a flow of material understandable by your student, you can meet one important mode of learning, memory.

Repetition helps the incorporation of the material into the student's long-term memory. In general, and greatly simplified, memory has two parts, one with a short term and another of longer term. Short-term memory holds information for a few minutes enabling important information to be assigned a space, ready for retrieval from the long-term memory. Repetition can provide a bit of extra time for your student's mind to complete this coding process.

Next, your course should be broken down into small pieces that can be put together in its final form, like a child's fort, which has been constituted of building blocks. Computers work well for this, but keeping simple by putting the parts and their descriptions on index cards is easy. I suggest that you label your cards as Administrative, Schedule, Content, or Assessment (see the following illustration).

To aid you in establishing an effective flow of information, while keeping you from getting lost in your own writing, I recommend the following relatively simple content card method. To begin, ask yourself an important question that is key to the subject you wish to teach. Once you have determined what this first primary question should be, ask yourself three additional secondary questions that will affect your instruction of the topic.

For instance, if your topic is about developing and solving proper equations, you may establish, "What components can be found in a good equation?" As your three supporting questions, you may ask: "How is an equation defined?", "What factors can be found in the equation?" and "What operations must be performed to arrive at the correct answer?"

You may put short statements answering your initial question on your cards always keeping them in a useful order. As you add to your pile, you can add more ideas and useful facts on additional cards. Continue your reviews and ordering them until you are satisfied that your opening questions have been answered.

Most courses consist of several, and often many, essential topics. Our equation example might include lessons on different types of equations such as binomial equations and trinomial equations. Your content cards should take the information being taught and broken down into smaller groups that describe the broader number of topics being studied. Put your cards into an order by lesson. Each lesson should become more detailed than the previous lesson. Typically, there are 12 to 16 weeks to a semester; this may differ depending upon your curriculum provider (see page 112).

You may now develop content to be taught within the time constraints required. It is time for you to establish your schedule cards. Take your piles of content cards and put them in place under your schedule cards, a card for each topic, lesson, week, or day so that you have what will be taught in each class period. Put those classes into a calendar order (see page 112).

If you are going to take the time to teach a course and expect your student to learn the material, you must be able to assess both your student's learning and your teaching effectiveness. To structure an effective assessment program using the card method, you must establish a series of assessment cards.

In Chapter 7 we discussed assessment. We talked about the need for effective assessment and both summative and formative methods. Write your assessment cards for each lesson using a method suitable for the topic being learned in that lesson and the requirements of your curriculum provider.

Your assessment cards for each class should be put beneath each lesson content pile. These cards will describe the means of assessment (see our Chapter 7 on assessment). You may ask yourself, "What results do I expect?" and "How should those results be tabulated?"

Remember, assessment is designed to meet the specific needs of your curriculum provider and testing consultant. Although I and most of my colleagues subscribe to formative assessment methods to determine student understanding, institutions and bureaucracies prefer summative methods, which are more objective and easily tabulated.

Administrative cards will contain the course name, when the course is given and how, what materials your student needs, the rules and boundaries in effect for the student while being taught, a statement of goals and objectives, and a description of the assessment procedure.

You should now have two piles in front of you. You will have one pile for each type of card: Administrative, Content, Schedule, and Assessment.

Once you have all these cards together, check their order, and write them down in a presentation format. There are many format templates that are available free online. Put your cards into the subject areas you need for your program. These subject areas may include Place, Schedule, Enrollment, Course Description, Materials, Rules or Expectations, Goals, and Objectives. There may be others or you may change the sub-titles, but that is of little meaning as long as the course structure is served.

Should you go through this whole process? The answer is quite simple. Yes. Take the time and do it right.

As homeschool parents, you are not professional educators. Nevertheless, it will be qualified educators who will approve your courses and authorize your testing suitable for presentation to employers and universities. Frankly, I want you to appear as skilled as possible. The best way to do this is to provide a product that looks practiced at the time of submittal.

Your Curriculum Presentation Process: Writing a Syllabus

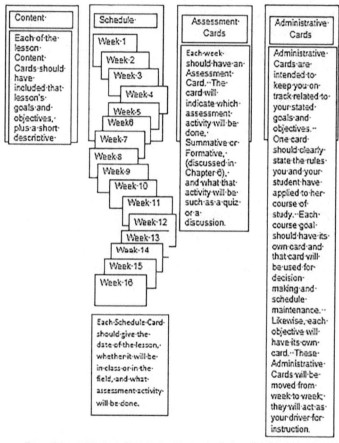

Content	Schedule	Assessment Cards	Administrative Cards
Each of the lesson Content Cards should have included that lesson's goals and objectives, plus a short descriptive	Week 1 Week 2 Week 3 Week 4 Week 5 Week 6 Week 7 Week 8 Week 9 Week 10 Week 11 Week 12 Week 13 Week 14 Week 15 Week 16	Each week should have an Assessment Card. The card will indicate which assessment activity will be done. Summative or Formative, (discussed in Chapter 6), and what that activity will be such as a quiz or a discussion.	Administrative Cards are intended to keep you on track related to your stated goals and objectives. One card should clearly state the rules you and your student have applied to her course of study. Each course goal should have its own card and that card will be used for decision making and schedule maintenance. Likewise, each objective will have its own card. These Administrative Cards will be moved from week to week; they will act as your driver for instruction.

Each Schedule Card should give the date of the lesson, whether it will be in-class or in the field, and what assessment activity will be done.

From these notes and cards it will be relatively easy for you to write your syllabus. Please see the following example from my personal

<u>**Example Syllabus**</u>

Train the Disaster and Emergency Preparedness Trainer

Certification:
This course will provide a corporate certificate for KSL Chile Pacific to all completing students.

Place:
This course can be taught in KSL Chile Pacific classrooms or in a client's suitable premises.

Duration:
The course is 40 hours in duration (5 eight-hour days) plus 1 hour each day for lunch. The maximum classroom size is 16 students.

Language:
The course, Train the Disaster and Emergency Preparedness Trainer will be given in Spanish and English.

Enrollment:
Students are expected to enroll at least one week, 7 days, before the start date. Each time a class approaches its maximum number of students, a new class registration will begin. KSL Chile Pacific can schedule multiple classes for clients with many applicants.

This course is intended for individuals that have a basic understanding of high-stress crisis situations or who have worked in a crisis, who hold a degree or have a related professional skill, such as firefighter or law enforcement officer, and who have related training experience as a trainer.

Course Description:
This course is presented as a series of case studies. Each case study will include discussion of several "Challenge

Questions" and a multiple-choice quiz on which a minimum score of 90% will be required. The case studies will include Hurricane Katrina, the Oklahoma City Bombing, the 27 February 2010 earthquake, and tsunami in central Chile, the Puyehue volcanic eruption in Southern Chile, and the Mount Pinatubo eruption in the Philippines. The students will receive additional instruction in classroom management, the process of learning, handling questions and inquiries, taxonomy, and exercises in-class presentations.

This is a senior level class dealing with highly technical issues. Those who do not qualify cannot be admitted.

Course Materials:
Each student will be provided with a student guide, pen, notepaper, and an appropriate, safe, and threat-free classroom environment. The student will have computer and internet access for research purposes.

Rules:
Each class will be assigned a specific starting time. Students are expected to arrive at the prescribed time.

Interference with or interruption of the class will not be tolerated and may be resolved by removal of the student from the class.

The student will be allowed to bring his/her own non-alcoholic drinks although drinks will be available for purchase at the training site.

No food will be allowed in the classroom.

No chewing gum or smoking will be allowed in the classroom.

Students will be expected to wear appropriate clothing and will not be expected to perform any activities dangerous to the student or his/her personal apparel.

No harassment of any kind between students will be tolerated.

No weapons will be allowed in class unless the student has preapproved duty requirements.

Photos, Recording, and Cellphones:
Cellphones will be turned off while the student is in the classroom. Airline mode is not acceptable.

No recordings, visual or sound, will be allowed without prior and specific permission of the KSL Chile Pacific Director.

Students will have adequate breaks, approximately ten minutes each hour, to make and receive phone calls.

Course Scheduling:
The goal of the case studies is to find commonalities upon which a foundation for good decision making for preparedness can be made. Since interaction between students is important to the class and key to preparedness, discussions will be allowed to overlap the days' schedules. It is more important to shorten another case study than to interfere with positive and constructive discourse.

Day 1: Hurricane Katrina
An introduction to the course's goals and objectives will open the class. Hurricane Katrina was an American disaster, which cost many lives and was filled with both proper and improper, good and bad, decisions and actions. In this, the student will assess the effects of those decisions. The students as a group will discuss in small breakout groups what

decisions should have been made and why. A short quiz will be given mid-day.

Day 2: The Oklahoma City Bombing and Chile's February 2010 Earthquake and Tsunami

One bright morning, 19 April 1995, in Oklahoma City, Oklahoma USA, Timothy McVeigh set off a large home constructed bomb in front of the Federal Building downtown. Hundreds were killed, including many children. Why did he carry out such an act? What were the ramifications in the community, even to this day?

The case study of the 27 February 2010 earthquake and tsunami in Chile will be discussed and assessed as to positive decisions and outcomes vs. negative decisions and outcomes. Since past decisions and outcomes weigh heavily in the preparedness realm, this discussion has many implications in the training process for future planners. A short quiz is planned.

Day 3: Completion of the 27 February Earthquake and Tsunami, the Puyehue and Mount Pinatubo Eruptions

The case study of the 27 February disaster will be finished and closed. The case studies about volcanic events will be presented. With two volcanoes at opposite ends of the globe, what were the similarities and differences between them? Their mitigation and remediation efforts will be discussed and appropriateness determined. A short quiz will follow.

Day 4: Classroom Management and Taxonomies

The trainer will find him/herself in classrooms with students from many walks of life and experience. As prospective instructors, the students must learn to manage groups large and small with both experienced and knowledgeable students as well as novices. All their students must be taught with care and consideration. Beginning with instruction on preparing a lesson plan, the lesson will discuss details for the use of taxonomies and student assessment.

The construction of a lesson plan will be taught. The students will prepare a short lesson plan on a topic of their choice and "teach" the class. After the presentations, there will be a debriefing to identify effective and ineffective techniques and why they were effective or ineffective. This is a learning activity geared toward future success, not a current failure for mistakes. Therefore, grades will NOT be given for the presentations.

Day 5: Teaching Methods, the Psychology of Learning, and Handling of Questions and Inquiries

This class is intended to provide the prospective instructor with several proven and effective tools that he/she can apply to an effective classroom. The student will be presented with several effective teaching techniques. In addition, he/she will receive instruction in the application of taxonomies and some concepts of the learning process and how the human mind learns as it does. The class will provide the prospective instructor with foundational material that will enable him/her to meet the challenges in a real classroom environment.

Lesson Plans

Be sure to write your lesson plans. Don't try to fake it, plan it.

Once you have your syllabus completed (for an experienced writer, this process will take about 2 days), you must prepare your lesson plans. There should be a lesson plan written for each item for which you have a content card. For instance, with your finished syllabus as discussed above, you will also create lesson plans for each day with a plan for every new or additional topic being taught. As a non-professional educator, you can consider a lesson plan as being your teaching detail, the words you say, and the activities you demonstrate, which your student copies.

Your lesson plans should include the following factors, at a minimum. Always feel free to add details as needed. While teaching a lesson, an instructor often wishes an additional factor or two to be covered as well. Feel free to add that information as needed. You can also remove unnecessary information. The question, "Why is that in here?" is often asked by a presenting instructor. Sometimes the information is inappropriate or unneeded. Other times the material should be presented elsewhere to maintain the proper flow of information. Again, feel free to make those changes. Your goals and objective will help you decide the correct course of action.

The following example lesson plan should give you an idea of a plan's construction. This example is an excerpt from my original course files, "Public Awareness in Disaster and Emergency Preparedness."

Example Lesson Plan Construction:

Awareness Lesson 1: Class Management, Goals, and Objectives

Duration:
1.5 hours with two 10-minute breaks at the discretion of the instructor.

Course Materials:
The student will need a copy of the 2008 Emergency Response Guidebook, U.S. Department of Transportation.

Goals:
This lesson is intended to provide the student with broad concepts of the breadth and regionalism of various types of threats in the maritime environment.

To accomplish this, comparisons are made of piracy and other events between the East and West coasts of Africa (found in your course text). In a demonstration of the global threat picture, we have taken real reports and descriptions of events in regions, which have typically been thought of as safe.

This lesson is being provided using a narrated PowerPoint presentation.

Objectives:
The student will:

- Explore the various types of threats found in Africa.
- Compare Africa's threats on both East and West coasts.
- Learn about the global aspects of maritime threats.
- Discuss the threat within the students' home country or operational regions.
- Become a more competent observer.

Instructors:
Assigned instructors are highly competent maritime and tactical professionals. Their responsibility is to provide the students with the knowledge to meet or exceed the course goals and to augment the prepared course with personal anecdotal information and experiences.

Content:
Include your content material here. Use one of two options. The first is a word-for-word representation of what you will teach. This will relieve you of depending on your memory while teaching an unfamiliar topic. The other option is to use an outline format. Outlines allow you some flexibility in your presentation and enable a smoother flow of information to your student. However, to use an outline format, you must be absolutely familiar with the topic at hand.

There are resources online for help in writing lesson plans from such websites as www.lessonplanet.com. I have provided an additional sample lesson plan taken from the internet. This sample is intended to demonstrate both differences that may be found in lesson plan formats and the variety of resources available.

[34]Sample High School Lesson Plan

AP Economics Lesson Plan: 10/24/2012

Objective: Communicate the idea of perfect competition by charting the four variables of the market (quantity of buyers/sellers, the existence of identical products, informance levels of buyers/sellers, and free market entry/exit) in accordance with products the students choose.
Time: 30 minutes
Materials: Laptops with Microsoft Excel, internet access, textbooks to check facts.
Procedure:

1. Ask students what they think "perfect competition" in economics would be. After a couple minutes of brainstorming, give them the dictionary definition: *A market in which all elements of monopoly are absent and the market price of a commodity is beyond the control of individual buyers and sellers.*
2. Now request that they give you examples of products they use relatively often: toothpaste, shoelaces, pepperoni pizza, etc.
3. Take several of these examples and draw a chart on the board like the one below, with the conditions of perfect competition at the top and the product names on the left. Have the students recreate this chart on their laptops using Excel.

---

[34] Taken from https://www.wikihow.com/Sample/High-School-Lesson-Plan

	Lots of Buyers/ Sellers	Identical Products	Informed Buyers/Sellers	Free Market Entry/Exit
Product #1				
Product #2				
Product #3				
etc.				

4. Divide the class into as many groups as you have sample products and assign each group a product to research. Give them roughly 10 minutes to do this. They must have at least 3 credible sources to confirm their findings.

5. Get a representative from each group to come up to the front of the board and record their conclusions (a yes/no in each column will suffice). Once all the products have been accounted for, discuss each conditional factor and whether or not the group's analysis of it is accurate. Make sure everyone adds the other products' information to their own charts, including notes of their own at the bottom if they like.

   Homework: Read through Chapter 18 of the textbook and answer questions 1–10 on page 263.

Note: Following the Appendices you will find information from The Center for Teacher Effectiveness, Time To Teach^{TM}. You will find many books that are guides for teaching a variety of differentiated instruction and classroom management topics. Within these are both complete lesson plans and directions. These materials can be ordered at www.cpr4classroommanagement.com.

Researching:

We have provided you with an understanding of the necessity of writing both a syllabus and related lesson plans. When homeschooling, even when you purchase a curriculum or course, it is you that must teach it. You must know what is on the course and what resources are available to help you teach it to your student successfully. That is the crux of this book.

Now that you have a handle on what goes into a course with its syllabus and lesson plans, I want to give you a few words about researching. When adding to or creating your own content, you must have an idea about how to proceed with your research to either write or understand course content. I'll try to make it easy by using the KISS principle, Keep It Simple Stupid; a principle I use all the time.

As I mentioned, there are three principle reasons that require content research. The first is to understand the content you are teaching. You may find yourself checking a dictionary or "Googling" on the internet seeking answers to questions you might have. The second is finding additional information to include in your purchased curriculum so that you can make it more interesting or both you and your student. The third purpose is to collect the necessary information you may need to create your own course. Some curriculum suppliers' assessment procedures will consider recognition of these elective courses.

When research is necessary, here are a few sources that are commonly available. We touched on them in our chapter about resources. Of the three to use that will do you the most good quickly are bookstores such as Barnes and Noble because you are able to peruse a book quietly even without buying it. If you decide you will need the book, then, by all means, buy it. Otherwise, take good notes. Remember, information that is not part of your personal knowledge or lexicon must be footnoted. These footnotes give credit to the originator, help your student or other interested persons find your source for their work, or provide enhancement or substantiation to your own work.

The second is the Internet. You may select the Internet as your first choice if you have a computer available. You must realize that the internet can provide you with access to huge volumes of information, but that does not ensure that the information you have received is accurate or truthful. Always seek more than one source. I generally use a minimum of three content sources and remove any references to information from suspect sources. Just as you would from information gathered from printed material, you must note what site you obtained your information found on the internet. I recommend that once you find a reference, print it so that you can prove your research and have readied the required reference, even in a "found in" reference that gives the URL (link).

The third is the public library. Most main libraries have the reference material needed, but due to the common use of the Internet, reference sections are getting smaller and less complete. Reference sections in branch libraries have typically become rather small due to financial constraints and the growing use of electronic sources. In some small neighborhood libraries, research sections have completely disappeared.

Many people without computers use the computer sections in their library for research. There is one problem with this and that is the computer stations must be shared. It often seems that just as you find what you are looking for, your allotted time is over.

One huge benefit of good reference sections is that the materials can often be borrowed and returned when done without cost. Also, most have highly trained professional librarians whose job is to assist you with your content searches.

Note: Remember all the material that you discover that isn't previously known by you must be referenced in your writing by a note in your content or a footnote. Take a look at the footnotes in this book for suitable examples. Your note should include the title, the date published, the author, the publisher, and where it was published.

When using the Internet, you will find information on almost any topic from hundreds of sources. Your challenge is to find and compare multiple sources.

Research is time intensive. Choosing a written format is important to help you with your research. Due to its formal structure in the presentation of the material, titled, subtitled, and numbered, a textbook format is often more useful than a prose structured or informal format. If you have a choice of a textbook or a less formal prose to find your information, choose the textbook.

There is a method I developed for research reading that has proven to be successful to a number of my students over the years. The method assumes that you own the book or you can usually buy such used books on Amazon and eBay for near pennies on the dollar. A new textbook priced over $60 may only cost $3$5 this way. The reason for choosing the textbook is the information has already been organized and indexed. (Please visit Appendix i: How to Read a Textbook for Content in One Weekend)

Self-Assessment Questionnaire

Did you read the entire chapter? Yes ☐   No ☐

List three things you got out of the chapter:

1.

2.

3.

How will you apply these things to teaching your student?

Congratulations on completing this chapter!

Chapter 9
Our Students and Their Needs

Before we get to your student in the next chapter, let's talk about the needs of every parents' students. Students you will never meet have a great deal to do with the scale by which your student will be measured.

It may sound a bit clichéd, but our students come in every shape and form, male or female, with positive and negative traits, and with a host of desires. Although all those who will judge your student, the education institution, society, and government, insist upon setting "norms" that are expected to be met by all students. This may have been an unfair indictment in some respects.

Caring and feeling people within the system have tried to meet the needs of students who fall into smaller groups, even groups of just a very few; however, it is in the grouping itself where the system fails and the homeschool parent shines. Bureaucracies must necessarily group people to provide the services they need. In that process, the individual is sometimes lost. It is for this reason that there are many learning advocates who try to individualize the learning duration and process as much as they are able.

Our students range from little more than toddlers to adolescents to young adults, to adults in college or continuing education. We are most concerned with the first three categories. Our students may have any number of physical, emotional, or mental challenges with which they must deal. They are not solely focused on their textbooks; nor do they think only of their studies and getting a high grade-point-average (GPA). They will meet challenges from social biases and prejudices as well. They will likewise be challenged by those who consider them as threats or competitors and even some who are unwelcome helpers.

To discuss "our students" meaningfully, we must fulfill our initial requisite of identifying categories of students, then provide a little discussion about each. It important to understand that I am an educator with a specific, though broad, background and do not have the same skills as a psychiatrist, psychologist, medical doctor, or lawyer. Instead, my goal is to acquaint you with the important student categories or types. It is to provide enough insight so that when you need to seek the services of an appropriate professional, you can do so with understanding and open eyes.

Let's Begin by Identifying Our Categories:

Note: Many sources consider physically, emotionally, and mentally challenged students under the same classification "special needs". I follow the perspective that each of these is different and separate, each with its own support requirements.

1. The physically challenged student
2. The emotionally challenged student
3. The mentally challenged student
4. The discipline problem student
5. The student with social challenges

There is a big hullaballoo going on today over inclusion. As a potential homeschool parent, and in fact, any parent, it is important to understand inclusion. It is one deciding factor on making your decision about whether to homeschool your student or not or whether you will react, pro or con about the issue.

Inclusion is the concept that for the social good of the individual student and all students, children should be included in the classroom, regardless of their challenges. Inclusion is very egalitarian, but I do not, by experience and observation, believe that overall it is a positive concept. Why do I feel as I do, and it's up to you to determine if you agree as it is your students' education that is affected? As an example, we have seen the classroom where an individual student was moved in on a medical gurney. What of the head and brain-injured students who sit in class but make little or no indication of their being in a learning process? Frankly, a classroom is not equipped to meet many of the needs of these children.

[35]We all want the best for our students. I, therefore, refer the reader to an article written in 1997 and updated in 2017 by Sharon Cromwell in Education World, which I feel represents the inclusion argument very well. The following are excerpts from that article. Please look the article up to read it in full.

Inclusion—the idea that all children, including those with disabilities, should and can learn in a regular classroom—has taken firm root in many school systems, although it is not specifically required by law.

'To oppose inclusion would seem to advocate exclusion. Yet, some observers maintain that full inclusion isn't always the best way to meet student needs. Critics of full inclusion ask whether even students with the most severe disabilities benefit from placement in regular classrooms.'
'What appears to be a major hurdle in the path to finding the proper method for inclusion is the fact that very few

---

[35] Article by Sharon Cromwell, Education World®, Copyright © 1997, 2017 Education World

major policy-making groups have addressed the issue in decades. The National Education Association (NEA), the largest and most powerful teachers' union in the U.S., displays its official stance on the topic, which the group approved in 1994.'

'Educators are not the only ones battling over inclusion. Not all parents of students with disabilities support the approach. Some parents fear to lose special education services they have fought for and believe their children will be "dumped" into regular classrooms without appropriate support.'

'Even the staunchest backers of inclusion recognize that it requires support services and changes in the traditional classroom. Here is a listing of provisions that must be met for inclusion to work best:

- [36]adequate supports and services for the student, well-designed individualized education programs
- professional development for all teachers involved, general and special educators alike
- time for teachers to plan, meet, create, and evaluate the students together
- reduced class size based on the severity of the student's needs
- professional skill development in the areas of cooperative learning, peer tutoring, adaptive curriculum, varied learning styles, etc.
- collaboration between parents, teachers, and administrators
- sufficient funding so that schools will be able to develop programs for students based on student need instead of the availability of funding, or lack thereof.'

---

[36]Utah Education Association, from http://www.myuea.org/blog.aspx

If these conditions are met, the fear of dumping students in regular classrooms becomes moot.

'[37]Federal law still requires that a full continuum of placement options be available to each special education student and that placement decisions be made by the Individual Education Program (IEP) team, based on the student's needs. Congress and the courts, however, have affirmed the legal right of children with disabilities to be educated in the least restrictive environment possible. To many, that means "full inclusion" with all students belonging in regular classrooms. To others, it means full inclusion for some children with disabilities and for other children with disabilities, a different approach.'

I, as you, want the best for all students, but that "best" is not the mere facts of age or grade level. The "best" is what benefits the class as well as the individual student. We want our students to be lifted and not held back or negatively affected. A high maintenance student forces a class's instruction to be obstructed while the included student with needs does not receive the support he or she may need.

What of socialization? The student with such needs must have a means of receiving the growth received from the establishment of human connections. Comparable programs are available, many through faith or non-profit organizations that are designed to meet such needs. It could be best to include more of these organizations directly through the classroom process.

The Physically Challenged Student

The physical challenges some students contend with may be resultant of illness, genetic disposal, accident, or social acceptance. I had a friend once who had a few physical challenges, which had limited his ability to interact in many

---

[37] Article by Sharon Cromwell, Education World®, Copyright © 1997, 2017 Education World

school activities. I had another friend whose genetic hip problem forced him into crutches and a harness arrangement that held up one leg. These boys suffered greatly from bullying. Unable to fight their own battles, I often had to fight theirs as well as my own since I was new in a small-town country school and being tested. Through these anecdotes, we can see that physical issues do affect the educational environment but also that social pressures can be equally as impactful for those students and others around them.

Public education has been at best poor in resolving such social problems, perhaps by lack of understanding, low prioritization, and response to political correctness or policy issues. In this case, what most educators do not seem to realize, that unlike law or regulation, the policy is made to be alterable or changeable to meet changing or developing needs.

'[38] Once we know what our goals for a child should be, we can draw on his many capabilities to help him achieve those goals. The motor system is not the only capability children have, and we can often take advantage of even limited motor ability.'

'If you can work around the limitations of his muscles and create situations that allow him to explore his own assertiveness, you will be helping him enormously. You might pair him up with another carefully chosen child, and find activities in which the boy with motor problems can be an assertive play partner. Although his speech is not always clear, he does have verbal skills.'

'The physically challenged child can get pleasure from creating along with his peers. Outdoors, if this child can't participate in a kickball game, you might encourage him to play with others in the sandbox. Encourage the children

---

[38] Working With Children Who Are Physically Challenged, Stanley I. Greenspan, M.D., 2017 Scholastic Inc.

there to create a drama with toys, using their voices rather than their bodies. Here again, you are helping the physically challenged child practice the skills he does have. Remember to always praise his efforts. The harder the task, the smaller the steps, and the greater the external rewards should be.'

'Teachers and parents should not be inhibited about their expectations of a child with physical challenges. In fact, they should capitalize on every opportunity that gives the child a sense of accomplishment.'

Working with the Emotionally Challenged Student

Like physically challenged students, emotionally challenged students can present some very interesting challenges for the parent or teacher. Emotionally challenged students can display their issues by acting out negatively or withdrawing from normal interactions with those around them. Sometimes, they may display an inordinately happy or carefree face. The key is they will act one way or another in ways different from the larger group or student norms. The homeschool parent or professional teacher must be observant or aware of these differences to ensure the student's effective learning.

[39]Working with emotionally and behaviorally challenged students lists some very pertinent tactics to be used that will help the homeschool parent as well as the teacher in the classroom.

Behaviors are intended to gain attention. Low-level bad behaviors may be ignored. Do not ignore higher-level

---

[39]Taken from, https://www.teachervision.com/working-emotionally behaviorally-challenged-students, Excerpted from Teacher Vision; *Back Off, Cool Down, Try Again: Teaching Students How to Control Aggressive Behavior*.

disciplinary issues. [40]The Time To Teach ™ program from The Center for Teacher Effectiveness (CTE) provides excellent professional training for dealing with disciplinary issues.

In both sources, the first for information and the second for training, generally agree and incorporate identifying signals given by students as to how they intend to act or act out. They agree in the proximity of the teacher to the student and a gentle touch in showing support in a non-threatening way. Public liability may dissuade a teacher in the classroom this closeness, but with a parent to a child, this tact should be both effective and bonding.

Changing the intensity of the lesson or the tempo of the presentation will provide a higher level of student motivation as will positive, but earned, comments. Connect with your student in a real way. This does not mean unearned praise or trying to be what you are not. Instead, it is being open to your student and letting her into who you are in a personal way, such as what your favorite flavor is or something about your last vacation.[41]Training in student motivation can be found with CTE.s, differentiated instruction program.

Not all your instruction is going to hit the mark. Be pragmatic in your review, fix it, and try again. Along those lines, get your student's opinion. What does he like about your teaching and what isn't working? Be prepared to avoid the errors and copy your successes.

As I stated earlier, a student will signal his acting or acting out. Watch those signals and change direction before his acting out begins. Remember students like meaningful routines. Note that changes can be routine as well when

---

[40] Center for teacher Effectiveness, Time To Teach ™, Rick and Aaron Dahlgren

[41] Center for Teacher Effectiveness, Differentiated Instruction, Eric Holmes

scheduled and purposeful. Support effective routine learning structures. While doing this, remember the KISS principle (Keep It Simple Stupid) and as you make your demands, changes, and schedules keep them as clear and attainable as possible. Confusion has no place in an effective learning process. Confusion does not equate to research.

The Mentally Challenged Student

Beyond not caring, there are no faults in dealing with mentally challenged students. Understanding is the platform you must work from. Mental issues can be myriad of type and effect. Limited intellectual capability to autism and such afflictions all occur and will continue to plague the innocent and those who take care of them. Each must have a professional evaluation of what actions and activities would be most valuable. [42] Tammy Reynolds, C.E. Zupanick, and Mark Dombeck provided us with a good guideline for the lay teacher dealing with students with intellectual disabilities in their 2013 article.

'Students with intellectual disabilities (ID, formerly mental retardation) benefit from the same teaching strategies used to teach people with other learning challenges. This includes learning disabilities, attention-deficit/hyperactivity disorder, and autism.'

'...break down learning tasks into small steps. Each learning task is introduced, one step at a time.

A second strategy is to modify the teaching approach.

A hands-on approach is particularly helpful for students with ID. They learn best when information is concrete and observed.

---

[42] Effective Teaching Methods For People With Intellectual Disabilities, Tammy Reynolds, B.A., C.E. Zupanick, Psy.D. & Mark Dombeck, Ph.D., May 21, 2013

Students with ID do best in learning environments where visual aids are used. This might include charts, pictures, and graphs. These visual tools are also useful for helping students to understand what behaviors are expected of them.

Provide direct and immediate feedback. Individuals with ID require immediate feedback. This enables them to make a connection between their behavior and the teacher's response.'

The Student with Social Challenges

I have found that social challenges in children are often linked to the challenges we discussed earlier in this chapter. However, for use in our chapter, we consider socially challenged students as a category of their own. You can watch several of my videos about this topic on my website http://www.rwt2015.con. They deal with such topics as dealing with real world talk, bullying, and youth suicide.

[43] Dr. Robert, in his presentation, Strategies to Support Social, Emotional, and Behavioral Needs of Students presents several ideas about dealing with socially challenged students. Dr. Weissberg lists risky youth behaviors as:

1. Physical fight one or more times (12 months): 31%
2. Carried a weapon (30 days): 17%
3. Bullied at school (past six months): 28%
4. Five or more drinks in a couple of hours (30 days): 24%
5. Seriously considered attempting suicide: 14%
6. Sexual intercourse with greater than three people: 14%
7. Chronically disengaged from school: 40–60%

---

[43] Strategies to Support Social, Emotional, and Behavioral Needs of Students, Roger P. Weissberg, PhD, University of Illinois at Chicago, March 11, 2011

He recommends to the student that she should:

- STOP, CALM DOWN, and THINK before you act
- Say the PROBLEM and how you FEEL
- Set a POSITIVE GOAL
- THINK of lots of SOLUTIONS
- THINK ahead to the CONSEQUENCES
- GO ahead and TRY the BEST PLAN

Social and Emotional Learning is a process of acquiring knowledge and skills related to five core competencies:

- Recognize one's emotions, values, strengths, and limitations
- Make ethical, constructive choices about personal and social behavior
- Form positive relationships, work in teams, deal effectively with conflict
- Show understanding and empathy for others
- Manage emotions and behaviors to achieve one's goals

The key to working with socially challenged students is that their behaviors are learned, often over years of observation or abuse. The fact is that the behaviors are intentional at some level. They have learned behaviors and can usually be unlearned or replaced. Some actions are defensive in nature while others have been learned, because there was no model available for proper behavior.

For the homeschool parent, I wish to throw a caveat in your direction, and it is an important one. There are some children that cannot be handled by anyone but a highly trained professional. I work at a school that specialized in working with the worst behavior problems in the state. I found that many of their parents were caring and hugely distraught by their child's actions. Some of these children were convicted of major violent crimes. I believe that most of these were a result of living within a drug culture, receiving acceptance by a violent group, or never having been expected to conform to normal social rules and boundaries. Sometimes love alone is not enough. If you are experiencing this as a parent, don't wait…seek help.

Self-Assessment Questionnaire

Did you read the entire chapter? Yes ☐ No ☐

List three things you got out of the chapter:

1.

2.

3.

How will you apply these things to teaching your student?

Congratulations on completing this chapter!

Chapter 10
Your Student

You made it. This is the last chapter and it is all about your student and getting her or him on the right path.

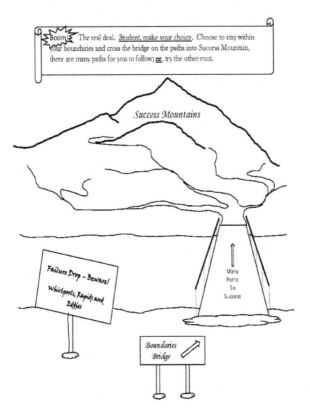

Step One: Know Your Student

Do you consider yourself a morning person or an afternoon person?

What do you enjoy writing about?

Tell me about a book you read.

How do you feel about being schooled at home?

What would special materials help make your learning easier?

What is your favorite food? How do you like it prepared?

These two questions are intended to open up a friendly discourse that will draw you both together. It is intended to be conversational rather than information gathering. Similar questions will work as well if the interview starts to become strained. We want to avoid any mutual contention if we can.

I went to _____ the other night and I_____. It was fun. Have you ever done that?

Questions like this will allow you to share a bit of yourself with your student by letting you be human, with your own likes and dislikes, rather than an automaton dealing only with directives, power, and instruction given. The student's learning in a home or small-group environment must be as a mentor, not as friends but caring.

What courses did you like most in the past?

How did your favorite teachers work with you?

Please, spend about five minutes and write a line of poetry you have made up.

This task will show willingness and your student's facility with words.

Have you read this book (showing the book)? Please choose two or three paragraphs and read them.

The task is to demonstrate the student's reading level. In our own home-school experience, our student, in the ninth grade, had difficulty with reading at a second-grade level. We spent hours reading, working on, and explaining Edgar Allen Poe's, The Raven. As a result, we never found him without a book and his reading grade level grew to a full ninth grade-level. This, by his own admission, turned his life around.

Note that the questions each had a purpose. None were threatening. All were intended to lead to a close teacher/student relationship.

Step Two: Write Your Goals and Objectives

Goals and Objectives

Primary Goals:	Secondary Goals:	Objectives:
Reach Success	•→ Complete this year with a B+ grade or better	1.→ 1-hour study each night in addition to homework
Have a happy Life		2.→ Follow curse guidelines
		3.→ Check at least two sources to confirm facts
Go to College		
	•→ Spend less money on stuff	1.→ Buy lunches offered at school
Get Married		2.→ Use the school stationary shop
Raise a family	•→ Make 2 new friends	Continue until you have a minimum of two objectives for each secondary goal.
	•→ Complete all my assignments	Each objective is a step to attaining your goal.
Make Money	•→ Join a club	
Primary, or long-term goals may relate to life goals or for short periods such as earning a degree.	•→ Help another student	Goals should be attainable but a challenge to meet. Therefore, the objectives should be well considered.
	Each secondary goal should be a waypoint on the way to meeting your primary, or long-term goals.	

Both the student and instructor should initial and date the final form as their commitment to meeting their goals. Not attaining a goal is not a failure, but it does require the establishment of another goal to replace it. We can learn a lot from failures we remedy.

Step Three: Establish Your Rules and Boundaries

Establish your rules and boundaries. These are the guidelines you will use to keep your studies on track day-by-day. I have listed a couple for you to begin with. Write the next boundaries and rules yourself. While you are taking into consideration your rules and boundaries, think about as rules to be, like regulations, statements to be followed as written.

These rules are subject to change by agreement. Boundaries, on the other hand, are socially oriented. Boundaries relate to generally accepted behaviors rather than performance issues. You can consider these as being the ethics statement of your program. The establishment of rules and boundaries is essential and should be written and initialed by both of you. Initialing is a statement of your acceptance.

<u>Sample Rules</u>
A minimum of one hour, in addition to instruction time and homework, will be used in the study.

Thirty minutes will be set aside each day for quiet reading.

I will keep a journal.

I will follow directions.

I understand that no threats will be made. If I act improperly, I will accept the discipline.

It is my study area; it is assigned to me. I will keep my study area clean.

<u>Sample Boundaries</u>
I will be home no later than 10:00 PM unless I have prior approval.

I will not curse or use abusive language.

I will use proper table etiquette.

I will dress neatly and keep myself clean.

Add other rules and boundaries, as you feel appropriate. Remember though, we want to make learning an interesting and enjoyable experience if we can. So don't overdo it in number or complexity. Again, refer to the KISS principal we discussed earlier.

Step Four: Give an Overview of Your Chosen Curriculum

By this time, you should have chosen which curriculum you wanted to follow. You have probably read its instructions and topical overviews and syllabi. If you are working with a public school, you have discussed with them your responsibilities and what they require. Read through the information and then sit with your student and discuss the application of the curriculum to him.

Discuss with the student the use of the study area you are providing and the responses expected to the provided curriculum. Introduce him to all his available materials, supplies, and training aids. Be sure to include the quiet space assigned to him. That noiseless space is essential; even if it's quiet time, it must be scheduled in a multi-use area.

My last words are direct to you. Teaching a homeschool student is work. You will also have a lot to learn. Hopefully, this book has gotten you firmly on that road.

There is no magic bullet; teaching takes time, preparation, patience, and understanding. If you are ready for it and up to it, homeschool teaching can be a more rewarding experience than you can imagine. It is both fulfilling and resulting in the creation of a loved one's future.

Good Luck.

<u>Self-Assessment Questionnaire</u>

Did you read the entire chapter? Yes ☐ No ☐

List three things you got out of the chapter:

1.

2.

3.

How will you apply these things to teaching your student?

Congratulations on completing this chapter!

Why We Teach What We Teach

Chapter 11
Why We Teach What We Teach Today:
History of American Education

American homeschooling is built upon a foundation of American education that dates back nearly four centuries. Remembering that at that time, America was a loosely knit group of British colonial proprietorships, which were primarily agricultural. Beyond leather goods, rum, and certain small metallic products, there was virtually no manufacturing industry. America was instead widespread in small family groups or villages, often facing great peril from hostiles, wild animals, a relatively unknown terrain, and extreme weather.

[44]As early as 1642, keeping in mind that the Separatists (Pilgrims) first landed in the New World in 1620, the Massachusetts Bay Company made a proper education mandatory in the colony. This became a model for other colonies as well.

There were some advantages that helped in establishing the American educational foundation as well. Facing an often wild, unsure, and dangerous environment produced a strong and independent population that had a tradition of education from their British Heritage. The interactions of marketing their products and the social aspects of local politics created

---

[44] Taken from, *"Schooling, Education, and Literacy, In Colonial America"* . faculty.mdc.edu. 2010-04-01.

generations of inquisitive, independent, and self-confident citizens.

[45]Education of the family children followed a pattern dating back to the ancient Greek Oikos (family). The Oikos was based upon the available labor force, a necessity when living a lonely existence on one of many widespread family farms. Here social interaction outside the family took place only on occasional trips to market in the nearest village and afternoons of drink and chat between males in the village inn.

To a modern woman, it may be uncomfortable that it was virtually a men's world off the farm. That was not a result of a masculine predisposition but instead the need to maintain the homestead. When on the farm in a family group, the family worked as a polished and organized unit. Assuming that a family consisted of children, parents, and grandparents, the young mother and father were generally responsible for running the farm including building the necessary shelters and buildings, planting, and harvesting.

Fathers and husbands went to market in the village and to catch up on the news of the day. Traveling to market was considered a significant challenge. During the First, and Second Great Awakenings (periods of growth and fervor in faith structures in the American 18th, 19th, and early 20th centuries that resulted in the denominational identification, influence, and growth), it was considered an essential duty of his to face the devils and temptations in the village.

[46]When not working alongside her husband, the young wife was considered responsible for running a Godly home

---

[45] Lawrence Cremin, *American Education: The Colonial Experience, 1607–1783* (Harper & Row, 1970)
[46] Taken from *"Schooling, Education, and Literacy, In Colonial America"*. faculty.mdc.edu. 2010-04-01.

ready to receive her husband returning from the market and providing him with relief from the stress of facing the devil's world found away from the home. This was an important and key function at the time. She was responsible for the healthcare of the family and became quite expert in the use of folk medicine, teaching the children basic cyphering (arithmetic), writing, and reading through the liberal use of scripture.

The children's responsibilities were to help with the care and feeding of the animals, to become literate at an elementary level, and to learn scripture. Girls were to help the mother around the house, while learning housekeeping techniques, cooking, and sewing. When of age, boys would be expected to learn heavy farm work in the fields with their father.

When the grandparents were still living, their primary job was to aid in the education of the children, often by anecdote and experiential stories. They were expected to help the mother maintain a Godly home and might watch the children enabling the mother to go to market with the father. Grandparents would assist in any way they could, given their age and physical capabilities.

[47] It is important to understand that the training and teaching of children was an essential part of frontier and farm life outside of the village structure.

---

web.archive.org/web/20110110043822/http://faculty.mdc.edu/jmc nair/Joe28pages/Schooling%2C Education%2C and Literacy in Colonial America.html

[47]Taken from,

http://faculty.mdc.edu/jmcnair/Joe28pages/Schooling, Education, and Literacy in Colonial America.htm

The Law of 1683 stated, '[48]Anyone having children in their charge MUST make sure that they could read and write by age 12.' The children were expected to be taught enough to enable them to conduct family business expected at that time. But, things were about to change, and change rapidly.

Education Moves to Town

[49]Sarah Roberts wrote in 2002 of the importance of women in teaching in 19th century America. She wrote in History of Education in the United States (2002) – Wikipedia:

> [50]'By the early 19th century, with the rise of the new United States, a new mood was alive in urban areas. Especially influential were the writings of Lydia Maria Child, Catharine Maria Sedgwick, and Lydia Sigourney, who developed the role of republican motherhood as a principle that united the state and family by equating a successful republic with virtuous families. Women, as intimate and concerned observers of young children, were best suited to the role of guiding and teaching children.
>
> By the 1840s, New England writers such as Child, Sedgwick, and Sigourney became respected models and advocates for improving and expanding education for females. Greater educational access meant formerly male-only subjects, such as mathematics and philosophy that were to be integral to curricula at public and private

---

[48] From,
http://scholarcommons.usf.edu/cgi/viewcontent.cgi?article=3684&context=etd

[49] Sarah Robbins, "The Future Good and Great of our Land': Republican Mothers, Female Authors, and Domesticated Literacy in Antebellum New England," *New England Quarterly* 2002 75(4): 562–591

[50] From,
https://en.wikipedia.org/wiki/History_of_education_in_the_United_States

schools for girls. By the late 19th century, these institutions were extending and reinforcing the tradition of women as educators and supervisors of American moral and ethical values.'

Growing Elitism in the Southern States

[51]Catherine Clinton (1982) expounded even further about the ideal of Republican motherhood and its place in American education. She wrote:

'The ideal of Republican motherhood pervaded the entire nation, greatly enhancing the status of women and supporting girls' need for education. The relative emphasis on decorative arts and refinement of female instruction, which had characterized the colonial era, was replaced after 1776 by a program to support women in education for their major role in nation building, in order that they become good republican mothers of good republican youth. Fostered by community spirit and financial donations, private female academies were established in towns across the South as well as the North.'

There were several teaching aids available for mothers at home on the frontier and teachers in the villages and cities. As would be expected, the principle book was the Holy Bible, Protestant in the English Colonies, and Catholic in the Spanish and French colonies. The most common textbook was the Hornbook. Hornbooks were common in the colonies and included The New England Primer (printed in Boston) used in Puritan communities and taught a Calvinist, which defined the authority of God, Jesus, and his parents.

The Industrial Revolution

---

[51] Catherine Clinton, "Equally Their Due: The Education of the Planter Daughter in the Early Republic," *Journal of the Early Republic* 1982 2(1): 39–60

The Industrial Revolution began in the U.S. during the last decade of the 18th century. With this, immigration grew and many young men and women moved into the cities and villages to make their fortune. [52]The related social and economic changes of the time forced a great change in education. In the village structure, most teachers were men, often ex-soldiers who could teach the 3 R's (readin', 'ritin', and 'ritmetic).

Payment of teachers in these early times was very low as teachers were initially expected to live in a provided home. Students were often sent to school with a few pennies in their pockets to pay the teacher for the day's courses. If these few pennies were not possible, teaching could be paid for through a barter system; 'You teach my child and we will give you a chicken.' This period of change began to be reflected in the face of American education.

[53]'The whole people must take upon themselves the education of the whole people and be willing to bear the expenses of it. There should not be a district of one-mile-square, without a school in it, not founded by a charitable individual, but maintained at the public expense of the people themselves.'

John Adams, U.S. President, 1785

The first public school, and first U.S. school was established in 1635 as the [54]Boston Latin School. The Boston

---

[52] Lawrence Cremin, *American Education: The Colonial Experience, 1607–1783* (Harper & Row, 1970)

[53]https://en.wikipedia.org/wiki/History_of_education_in_the_United_States

[54] Taken from, *"History of Boston Latin School—oldest public school in America"*. BLS Web Site.

Latin School remains in operation today. [55]The first free, taxpayer-funded public school in the United States is the Mather School established in Dorchester, MA, in 1639. The Mather School is also still active. [56]The first high school was opened in Boston in 1821.

[57] Per Paul Monroe, A Cyclopedia of Education (4 vol. 1911), As Americans relegated the Revolutionary War to history by starting a new country in 1789, the United States of America, they began to elevate the need for proper education to a higher priority. By 1870, every state had tax-subsidized elementary schools. This pattern would be followed in every state since then. [58]The U.S. had the highest literacy rate in the world by 1800, exceeding 90 percent in some regions.

Such education innovators as [59]Ellwood Patterson Chubberly (1868–1941) began to identify the need for professionalism in teaching and working to implement these new concepts into the larger educational institution. These changes helped education to become an institution with professional teachers, administrators, and standards.

American education had been built upon the traditions of colonialism and a widespread agricultural economy that had been rapidly changed to accommodate the requirements of

---

[55] Taken from, The Mather School is marking 375 years of public education; NYPD's Bratton, an alumnus, to speak at assembly | "Dorchester Reporter". www.dotnews.com

[56] Jurgen Herbst, *The Once and Future School: Three Hundred and Fifty Years of American Secondary Education* (1996)

[57] Paul Monroe, *A Cyclopedia of Education* (4 vol. 1911)

[58] Hannah Barker and Simon Burrows, eds. *Press, Politics and the Public Sphere in Europe and North America 1760–1820* (2002) p. 141

[59] Lawrence A. Cremin, *The Wonderful World of Ellwood Patterson Cubberley* (1965)

America's entry into the Industrial Revolution. [60]Some historians sought to begin a new and modern history of American education that includes such facets as professionalism, the meeting of modern social requirements, greater governmental involvement, and standardization.

[61,62]James McLachlan and Arthur Powell wrote about the early establishment of private high schools in Massachusetts in the 19th century, meeting some of the new needs of education during the Industrial Revolution. 'Early 19th century New England private high schools, today called "prep schools", including such institutions as Phillips Andover Academy (1778), Phillips Exeter Academy (1781), and Deerfield Academy (1797). They became the major feeders for Ivy League colleges in the mid-19th century. [63] These prep schools became coeducational in the 1970s, and remain highly prestigious today.'

Massachusetts was not the only colony to establish essential education in North America and in what is now the United States of America. [64]A leading colonial school was the Ursuline Academy in French New Orleans. It was established by the Catholic Church's Sisters of the Order of Saint Ursula in 1727. Woman leaders in Pharmacy and Literature are among its early graduates.

---

[60] Peterson, Paul E. (2010). Saving Schools: From Horace Mann to Virtual Learning. pp. 21–36. Messerli, Jonathan (1972). Horace Mann: A Biography

[61] James McLachlan, *American Boarding Schools: A Historical Study* (1970)

[62] Arthur Powell, *Lessons from Privilege: The American Prep School Tradition* (Harvard UP, 1998

[63] Ronald Story, "Harvard Students, The Boston Elite, And The New England Preparatory System, 1800–1870," *History of Education Quarterly,* Fall 1975, Vol. 15 Issue 3, pp. 281–298

[64] Clark, Robenstine. "French Colonial Policy and the Education of Women and Minorities: Louisiana in the Early Eighteenth Century," *History of Education Quarterly* (1992) 32#2 pp. 193–211

[65]Sol Cohen (1900–1976) was one of those early historians that sought to write a new history of American education. [66]He argues (1976) that, '…a rich and controversial chapter in the history of the education has been forgotten in the zeal to get on with the "new" history.' He contends that historians need to come to terms with the struggles, primarily in the 1930s and 1940s, between those who would make the field purely "functional"—addressed to teacher training and to contemporary social problems—and those who would make it an academic discipline. After tracing the development and context of those struggles, Cohen concludes by noting certain dangerous continuities between the past and the present in the craft of history of education. He cautions that progress can be made only by acknowledging and understanding that past.[67]

So begins a new history of American Education. Politics, organization, standardization, public funding, and social pressures take preeminence for education across the country rather than dictation by the practical division of labor.

[68] 'In earlier times, as American education began to distinguish itself, but before modern standardization and qualification, American teachers were not trained to teach. Being literate and experienced was often enough to teach. Hired by local school boards, tax income was often the deciding factor about who would be hired rather than qualifications, or even if a full-time teacher would be hired at all. Young single females were often preferred to keep

---

[65] Sol Cohen (*1976*), The History of the History of American Education, 1900–1976: The Uses of the Past. Harvard Educational Review: September 1976, Vol. 46, No. 3, pp. 298–330.
[66] Taken from
https://doi.org/10.17763/haer.46.3.gp631173780x511j
[67] From, https://eric.ed.gov/?id=EJ152811
[68] Jurgen Herbst, *The Once and Future School: Three Hundred and Fifty Years of American Secondary Education* (1996)

expenses as low as possible. In 1923, two "normal schools" (normal schools specialized in training teachers) opened to provide career paths for single middle-class women. This was a time when being female and unmarried often forced a woman into a service line of work such as seamstress, laundress, nurse, or even prostitute. Normal schools became the most effective means of teacher training by 1900.'

In the later 19th century and continuing until today, the United States education system had been guided by progressivism. Such people as John Frederick Dewey and Horace Mann significantly influenced progressivism in American education. It appears that early progressivism grew American education into a worldwide model for modern teaching. But current changes in the precepts of progressivism have left its original intent behind and in many cases replaced it by a self-servicing ethic.

Entering the Progressive Era

[69]Horace Mann (1796–1859) could be considered as one of the earliest educational philosophers that affected the inception of the progressive movement in education. He worked to establish a system of professional teachers following the Prussian system. The Prussian model, known also as the common-school system, sought to teach all students to the same criteria. In this model, students were placed in grade levels by age regardless of aptitude. This necessitated the training of teachers into an acceptable competency. His idea of universal public education evolved into what is referred to as the "factory model school".[70] The characteristics of this factory model include top-down

---

[69] Peterson, Paul E. (2010). Saving Schools: From Horace Mann to Virtual Learning. pp. 21–36. Messerli, Jonathan (1972). Horace Mann: A Biography

[70] Taken from, *The Impact of the Factory Model of Education in Central Texas*, abstract, Kelsey Leigh Stokes, Baylor University, 2013

management, separation from the community, emphasis on behavior and school management, centralized planning, standardization, outcomes designed to meet societal needs, and efficiency in producing results.

[71]John Dewey (1859–1952) was a leader in the pragmatist movement. The pragmatist movement had a substantial effect on educational progressivism for a short while. The pragmatist movement demonstrated that many influences affected the progressive movement in education. This movement was involved with the application of philosophy and thought to education. It had a great deal of influence in the progressive growth in education. He, John Dewey (1916), wrote his *Democracy and Education: An Introduction to the Philosophy of Education*, which argued that the combined knowledge of the larger group exceeded the capabilities of any individual within the group. [72]Therefore, a well-considered effort to educate the whole group is necessary.

[73]The late 19th century saw the rise in the Progressive Movement in America. The movement sought to reform social ills through public education. Large numbers of schools were built serving a growing population and offering a more advanced curriculum. With mandatory attendance, the number of students who had some advanced education grew dramatically.

[71] Dewey, John (1916). *Democracy and Education: An Introduction to the Philosophy of Education*.

[72] Peters, Michael. "Ecopolitical Philosophy, Education And Grassroots Democracy: The return' Of Murray Bookchin (and John Dewey?)." Geopolitics, History and International Relations, vol. 9, no. 2, Addleton Academic Publishers, July 2017, p. 7.

[73]Taken from, http://www.educationnews.org/education-policy-and-politics/american-public-education-an-origin-story

[74]According to Jurgen Herbst, the Progressive Movement extended from the 1890s to the 1930s. This period saw tremendous growth in a number of schools and successful graduates with high school diplomas. However, I would argue that the Progressive Movement became federalized during the administration of Woodrow Wilson and has been extended to the present. I would also argue that the Progressive Movement has begun to collapse under populist pressure and that the growth and recognition of educational alternatives of which homeschooling, parochial schools, and charter schools lead the pack.

[75]According to Plank and Peterson (1983), through the late 1890s, schools were built, teachers needed to meet higher standards, and labor organizations began to press for tenure. Reforms, as were the practices of the day, were meant to service the white community. Elitism grew by the middle-class professionals of that day toward much of the public including working-class members, traditional business elites, and certain ethnic groups. This elitism is felt even today.

The year 1929 was a pivotal year in world economies; the United States along with most of the world entered the Great Depression. With the general economic failure of the country, Plank and Peterson (1983), the Roosevelt administration's New Deal created many programs to hire the unemployed by providing jobs for building infrastructure. Schools and schooling were part of these programs that included the CWA (Civil Works Administration) and FERA (Federal Emergency

---

[74] Jurgen Herbst, *The Once and Future School: Three Hundred and Fifty Years of American Secondary Education* (1996)

[75] Plank, David N.; Peterson, Paul E. (1983). "Does Urban Reform Imply Class Conflict? The Case of Atlanta's Schools". History of Education Quarterly. 23 (2): 151–173

Relief Administration) [76] Leuchtenburg (1986). The programs resulted in the building or upgrading of over 40,000 schools for rural regions, and adult training and education. This resulted in the hiring of up to 50,000 teachers in both rural and adult education settings.

[77]Unfortunately, the New Deal did not provide funds for impoverished students, Kevin P. Bower (2004). But it did support technical and work-study programs that were open to both genders. As revenues fell, school districts were badly hurt during the Great Depression. Available funding was shifted to the various relief projects that did not service the established and financially stressed urban schools. President Roosevelt did not like or engage closely with progressive educators, who, in his opinion, were the elitists of the educational institution. All direct funding was refused to urban public schools, private schools, and colleges alike.

Homeschooling Across the Country

The elitism of many in the traditional educational institution in the U.S., as well as the curricular standardization demanded by a liberal government, and the tenure issues created by education's labor organizations, have forced many in the public to seek alternative methods for the education of their children.

While as a group, educators care greatly about the children put in their charge for education; there are still many who tend to play the "I know something you don't" education card when interacting with parents and other non-professionals. Many parents experience this the moment they must deal with administrators about their children or with their school board about community or curriculum issues. As

[76] Leuchtenburg, p 121–22; Tyack et al. Public Schools in Hard Times (1986) pp. 105.

[77] Kevin P. Bower, "'A favored child of the state': Federal Student Aid at Ohio Colleges and Universities, 1934–1943." History of Education Quarterly 44.3 (2004): 364–387.

a parent, I did, and as an educator, I have observed and experienced these biases.

Governments often want to control all facets of education under the premise that it is best for the children and will result in a more effective labor market. Because bureaucracies want neat and easy statistics, they combine their need to control with such programs as the Common Core Curriculum, which was originally designed to meet the needs of a particular state or school community[78]. This curriculum mandates that ALL children meet certain guidelines in a grade or age perspective rather than a developmental and abilities perspective. Many teachers believe that governmental controls, often to cure social ills, actually keep them from teaching properly while NOT having the desired effects in social arenas.

Fortunately, some authoritative members of government and education have come to recognize these issues and are seeking to remedy them. There was recently a push to stop the teaching of cursive in some schools. In fact, many schools have already stopped teaching it. Taking away cursive does not reflect the idea that electronic means are more often used today by students. Instead, it takes away a bit of the student's birthright. All of our foundational documents are written in cursive including the Declaration of Independence and the Constitution of the United States of America, not to mention key document dating back to the Magna Carta. In other words, an untaught student must go to a politician or attorney for information about his or her rights rather than being able to read them for his or herself. Also, the [79]Common Core Curriculum is being removed by many states.

---

[78] From,
https://www.usnews.com/news/special-reports/articles/2014/02/27/the-history-of-common-core-state-standards
[79] Refer to: http://www.corestandards.org/

Unions, Lobbying, and the Homeschooling Alternative

There are a number of teachers' unions. The two principal national unions are the American Federation of Teachers (AFT) and the National Education Association (NEA). Both are national with local associates. I do not intend to praise or detract from these. Instead, I hope to present a conflict between the union's perspective and homeschooling.

I am a firm believer in local teachers' unions. I have seen their work and the positive effect on teachers, students, and communities. At the same time, I have noticed many negatives within the national labor organizations, as their perspective appears centered around advancing tenure benefits, protecting poor teachers, and the establishment of a system that enables them to control education at all levels. The national organizations such as the NEA and AFT stand definitively against homeschooling.

They have no effective argument as to why they are so reticent. Their stated reasons tend to indicate that their reticence relates to their inability to control parental education.

I am not the only person to observe and write about the issue between the conflict between homeschool parents and the NEA. I offer the following written by [80]Julie Foster in her article NEA vs. homeschools. The NEA opposes nearly every aspect of parental-directed education. To summarize, she writes that the NEA Resolution B-68, adopted in 1988, was recently reaffirmed at its national convention.

Ms. Foster writes (2000), 'Resolution B-68 states: Homeschooling should be limited to the children of the

---

[80] Taken from http://www.wnd.com/2000/09/4581/, by Julie Foster, NEA vs. home schools Union opposes nearly every aspect of parent-directed education
Published: 09/10/2000 at 1:00 AM

immediate family, with all expenses being borne by the parents/guardians. Instruction should be by persons who are licensed by the appropriate state education licensure agency, and a curriculum approved by the state department of education should be used.

'The Association also believes that homeschooled students should not participate in any extracurricular activities in the public schools,' the resolution continues.

She goes on with an interview with NEA spokesperson Kathleen Lyons. According to Ms. Foster, Ms. Lyons stated that the NEA did not have an 'expert on homeschooling, and that it did not track homeschooling but said the statement has been the "long-standing position of the association".' In other words, one could say that the NEA may have indulged its ignorance through its elitist prejudices against homeschooling. The statistics do not support this NEA position.

[81]The NEA Spokesperson also said, 'It's our feeling that public schools are the best choice for parents. What we want to do is to ensure that that truth is more than our belief—that it is a fact.' It is true that there are many excellent public schools even that most public schools serve their communities well. But as the term "best choice" may not be true for all families and all children, the statement should perhaps indicate that public schools are most often a viable choice.

Moreover, Lyons stated that, 'Public schools have a wider variety and higher quality of courses for students to take such as advanced placement science courses, which are not as common in private schools.' It takes a person only minutes to research the wide variety of home and alternative schooling available to families and their students to find that this

---

[81] http://www.wnd.com/2000/09/4581/

statement is not factual. [82]The NEA is a lobbying union that operates within a highly regulated industry. Their statement is intrinsically incorrect and appears based upon their biases and incorrect or incomplete prejudices. According to their own comments, they do not track such things.

Along these same lines, the Spokesperson (Lyons) further stated, 'there is[83] "no question that public schools have better course offerings" than private schools.'

I fully disagree with her next statements, 'As for homeschools, no one parent can provide the high quality of education available at public schools,' she said, quickly adding, 'which is not to say a parent cannot adequately teach his child at home.' This book paints an entirely different picture, as there is a myriad of excellent resources available to parents seeking alternatives for their children. Those available statistics indicate that the alternatives are most often more effective than the public venue.

Ms. Foster responded to the NEA Spokesperson's position saying, 'I think the public school is a cafeteria plan,' also 'Public school students are instructed in Cooking and Sex Ed instead of reading, writing, and arithmetic anyway.' I believe that while her statement holds true for some public school districts, for the most part, public schools and their administrators and teachers have a sincere desire to teach our children. But they are often forced to teach curricula that are forced upon them by the political agendas of lobbying organizations.

Conversely, [84]Phyllis Schlafly, a family rights activist, presents different observations. The founder of *The Eagle Forum* says that, 'Homeschool students do not stay inside all

[82] Refer to:

http://www.opensecrets.org/industries/indus.php?ind=L1300

[83] http://www.wnd.com/2000/09/4581/

[84] Refer to *The Eagle Forum*, The Phyllis Schlafly report website at: http://eagleforum.org/publications/psr/aug15.html

day.' Instead, she says about parents that, 'They take them to the museums, they take them to the library, and they take them out for science fairs.'

As experienced homeschool grandparents, we certainly agree. Our grandson was often doing projects outside the home (in our case our 42' sailboat), using such resources as museums, libraries, and bookstores each week and often on a daily schedule. Environmental projects in the field were a regular part of his schedule. Our courses also included the fundamentals of reading and creative writing as well as mathematics, literature, history, Science, and government, with an opportunity to meet with peers, mainly other live-a-board sailing teens who were also being homeschooled. It is possible to homeschool nearly anywhere and under a wide variety of circumstances.

Ms. Foster makes an excellent point about the cost of homeschooling, 'The homeschool parents are paying the same school taxes that the other schools' children's parents are paying. I see no reason why they can't enjoy some of the benefits of public schools since they are participating in the funding of those programs,' she continued. 'Homeschool parents pay for public schooling and often pay for their homeschool resources as well.' Homeschool students should have access to the extracurricular activities in the public schools and many curricular resources as well. They paid for it as much, or more, than the parents of classroom students do.

This chapter is not intended to express personal preferences or an ethical statement. It is intended to provide the parents of homeschool students, or those seeking a greater understanding for the education process in America, with a background and information enabling them to make the best choices for the education of their students. Every student is different and there are available a wide variety of teaching modalities to meet those differences.

<u>Self-Assessment Questionnaire</u>

Did you read the entire chapter? Yes ☐ No ☐

List three things you got out of the chapter:

1.

2.

3.

How will you apply these things to teaching your student?

Congratulations on completing this chapter!

Appendices

Appendix i: How to Read a Textbook for Content in One Weekend

If you have a choice of a textbook or a less formal book written in prose to find your information, choose the textbook. There is a method I developed for research reading that has proven to be successful to a number of my students over the years. The method assumes that you own the book or you can usually buy such used books on Amazon and eBay for near pennies on the dollar. A textbook priced over $60 new may only cost $3–$5 this way. The reason for choosing the textbook is the information has already been organized and indexed.

When reading a book that uses prose-oriented writing, you must first organize the material for easy perusal. Textbooks are highly organized, usually into chapters, titled and subtitled content areas, and marked with numbering or lettering systems. This takes the burden of organization out of the hands of the parent enabling her to dive straight into reading for content.

When reading such a book (once you get the knack, you will be able to read an entire 350-page textbook for content in less than a weekend), begin with a skim of all pages and look at the pictures and illustrations with their comments. Do not read the content word-for-word in this initial skim. Let your mind pick out what it feels is unfamiliar to you. The intent of this initial skim is for you to get an idea of where information is presented that you are not familiar with.

The secret of this method I am presenting to you is for you to read only what you don't know. If you already know it, why would you need to study it again? You will skim, not read word-for-word, through the book reading the titles, subtitles, and captions, glance at the pictures and illustrations. Now we come to an essential; as you skim through the book, highlight the information you don't know with a light-colored highlighter.

After you have finished with this initial skimming, begin skimming again from the beginning, marking only what you now know with a slightly darker highlighter. Again, when done go through the process once more. By the time you finish the third skimming, you will find that your highlighting color is beginning to turn to brown because of the overwritten colors. You will also find that the brown highlighted lines are few and shorter than are the lines with lighter colors. This is because you are learning the content and the color changes have become an assessment process indicating your own growth in the topical knowledge. After your skimming is complete, take your notes on the subject on one of your index cards that can be put into your lesson plan or be presented directly to the student.

Appendix ii: Ideas for the Student to Simplify Report Writing

Objective means of assessment can be effective and are sometimes necessary. However, there is no replacement for the written essay and an occasional research paper. The ability of a student to understand the taught content, to organize her thoughts and present them in a clear and concise report is the meeting of a primary student goal usually stated in the syllabus.

Students often have difficulty identifying where they want to start in their report or paper. This difficulty is often persistent throughout the student's work on their paper. The method I recommend in this appendix resolves this issue and the issue of helping student writers stay on topic as they are getting to their point.

At some level, stated or unstated, reports, essays, and research papers begin with a question. Therefore, the student should begin with a question, which is followed by subordinate questions and their answers until the student's point is made. The following describes how this may be accomplished keeping in mind that the intention of this method is to aid the student in defining his topic and structuring an appropriate answer and…the method works. In writing:

1. The student defines a general question of interest to her and begins the paper by simply asking the question, or implying it, in the opening paragraph. This question should be in an open-ended form. An open-ended question form asked in a way that it requires a complex answer. It is often a "how" or "why" question. You cannot answer the open-ended question with a single world.

2. The student should make a statement about how she will answer the question, "I will answer this question by…" She should identify at least three points in answer to the question. I was advised one time that it should be seven points or more, but this could be excessive until the student becomes much more familiar with the method.

3. Subordinate questions may be open or closed-ended depending upon the answers being sought. A close-ended question expects a response of one or just a few words, i.e., 'What time did the event take place?' 'Resources indicate that the event took place at 3:00 AM.' As each point is answered, the next point is assigned an identified subordinate question, thereby tying the answers together in an easy flowing paper that stays on track.

4. Once all the subordinate questions have been answered, the student summarizes the answers with a statement of the answers related to the original question.
5. The student closes the paper with a statement that indicates that she has answered the original question by...and therefore... an ending statement of fact or completion.

Note that questions may be stated in question form or may be implied through a statement and description. Implied questions are stronger but usually need more experience or comfort with the method.

The intent of this book has been to assist homeschool parents in establishing an effective learning environment geared toward the success of their students. Secondarily, parents whose children are enrolled in more traditional means of education in public, charter, and parochial schools often find it necessary to work with or even confront actors in the educational institution. These actors may be positive or negative. Fortunately, positive educators by far outnumber the less capable, negative, rude, or unconcerned members of the institution. Teachers want to teach to their students' success. At the time, a teacher-parent team is needed. This book will help every parent with this interaction.

Appendix iii: List of Sources
1. Home School Legal Defense Association, Legal Research Supplement, Academic Statistics on Homeschooling, J. Michael Smith and Michael P. Farris, October 22, 2004
2. Home School Legal Defense Association, Legal Research Supplement, Academic Statistics on Homeschooling, J. Michael Smith and Michael P. Farris, October 22, 2004
3. Home School Legal Defense Association, Legal Research Supplement, Academic Statistics on

Homeschooling, J. Michael Smith and Michael P. Farris, October 22, 2004

4. The Bob Jones University Testing Service of South Carolina
5. Research Facts on Homeschooling, Brian D. Ray PhD., March 23, 2016, National Home Education Research Institute.
6. Homeschool Statistics: What Research Reveals About Homeschooling, Laura Powell, 5/15/2014, Bright Hub Education
7. Interview with Glenna M. Kuhlman, August 2017, Presidential Award in Teaching Elementary Mathematics, Contributor to the New Jersey Mathematics Standards; recognized expert in teaching the gifted and Talented Student.
8. Dr. Madeline Hunter (1982), The Madeline Hunter Model of Mastery Learning
9. Wood, D., & Wood, H. (1996). Vygotsky, Tutoring and Learning. Oxford Review of Education, 22(1), 5–16.
10. Tulane University, Tips for Writing Goals and Objectives, www.tulane.edu
11. Eric Combs, Dr. Aaron Dahlgren, and Dr. Diane I.M. Wittig, Time To Teach, Differentiated Instruction: Engagement and Motivation in Every Classroom, May 2014, Hayden Lake, ID, Center For Teacher Effectiveness. (page 6)
12. Taken from, Toastmaster International, Five Speaking Points, https://www.toastmasters.org/Find-a-Club/05282335-talkingpoints
13. Taken from, Toastmaster International, HAIL, https://www.toastmasters.org/Find-a-Club/05282335-talkingpoints
14. Fischer, D., & Frey, N. (2003). Writing instruction for struggling adolescent readers: A gradual release model. Journal of Adolescent & Adult Literacy, 46(5), 396–405.

15. Anderson, D. M., & Haddad, C. J. (2005). Gender, voice, and learning in online course environments. Journal for Asynchronous Learning Networks. 9, 3-14.

16. Jay Patterson (1999). Female Perception vs. Male Perception pg. 1, para. 4

17. Jay Patterson (1999). Female Perception vs. Male Perception, pg. 1, para.6

18. Jay Patterson (1999). Female Perception vs. Male Perception, pg. 1, para. 8

19. Jay Patterson (1999). Female Perception vs. Male Perception

20. Clark DR (1999), Bloom's Taxonomy, Learning Strategies or Instructional Strategies, retrieved from http://www.nwlink.com/hrd/strategy.html

21. Clark DR (1999), Bloom's Taxonomy, Learning Strategies or Instructional Strategies, retrieved from http://www.nwlink.com/hrd/strategy.html

22. Revans, R. W. 1998. ABC of action learning. London: Lemos and Crane.

23. Ellis, Wagner, & Longmire, 1999), Managing Web-based training: How to keep your program on track and make it successful. Set of Learner-centered Principals for Training, Alexandria, VA: ASTD Press

24. Fischer, D., & Frey, N. (2003). Writing instruction for struggling adolescent readers: A gradual release model. Journal of Adolescent & Adult Literacy, 46(5), 396–405.

25. Hunter, Madeline. (1984). Knowing, Teaching, and Supervising.

26. Groundwater-Smith, S., Le Cornu, R. J., & Ewing, R. A. (1998). Teaching: challenges and dilemmas: Harcourt Brace

27. University of Texas at Austin, Faculty Innovation Center © 2016–2017

28. University of Texas at Austin, Faculty Innovation Center © 2016–2017

29. Harlen, W. and James, M., (1997), Assessment and Learning: Differences and Relationships between Formative and Summative Assessment, Assessment in Education: Principles, Policy & Practice, 4(3): pp. 365–379.
30. K. Lambert of OCPS Curriculum Services (4/2012)
31. Bloom's Taxonomy, Benjamin Bloom, 1949
32. Taken from https://www.uhs.uga.edu/sleep, University of Georgia, University Health Center
33. College Textbook Prices Increasing Faster Than Tuition And…
    Downloaded from,
    www.huffingtonpost.com/2013/01/04/college-textbook-prices-increase_n_2409153.html
34. Taken from
    https://www.wikihow.com/Sample/High-School-Lesson-Plan
35. Article by Sharon Cromwell, Education World®, Copyright © 1997, 2017 Education World
36. Utah Education Association, from http://www.myuea.org/blog.aspx
37. Article by Sharon Cromwell, Education World®, Copyright © 1997, 2017 Education World
38. Working With Children Who Are Physically Challenged, Stanley I. Greenspan, M.D., 2017 Scholastic Inc.
39. Taken from,
    https://www.teachervision.com/working-emotionally-behaviorally-challenged-students,
    Excerpted from Teacher Vision; Back Off, Cool Down, Try Again: Teaching Students How to Control Aggressive Behavior.
40. Center for teacher Effectiveness, Time To Teach [TM], Rick and Aaron Dahlgren
41. Center for Teacher Effectiveness, Differentiated Instruction, Eric Holmes
42. Effective Teaching Methods for People With Intellectual Disabilities, Tammy Reynolds, B.A.,

C.E. Zupanick, Psy.D. & Mark Dombeck, Ph.D., May 21, 2013

43. Strategies to Support Social, Emotional, and Behavioral Needs of Students, Roger P. Weissberg, PhD, University of Illinois at Chicago, March 11, 2011

44. Taken from *"Schooling, Education, and Literacy, In Colonial America"*. faculty.mdc.edu. 2010-04-01.

45. Lawrence Cremin, *American Education: The Colonial Experience, 1607–1783* (Harper & Row, 1970)

46. Taken from *"Schooling, Education, and Literacy, In Colonial America"*. faculty.mdc.edu. 2010-04-01. web.archive.org/web/20110110043822/http://faculty.mdc.edu/jmcnair/Joe28pages/Schooling%2C Education%2C and Literacy in Colonial America.html

47. Taken from, http://faculty.mdc.edu/jmcnair/Joe28pages/Schooling, Education, and Literacy in Colonial America.htm

48. Taken from, http://scholarcommons.usf.edu/cgi/viewcontent.cgi?article=3684&context=etd

49. Sarah Robbins, "'The Future Good and Great of our Land': Republican Mothers, Female Authors, and Domesticated Literacy in Antebellum New England," New England Quarterly 2002 75(4): 562–591

50. From, https://en.wikipedia.org/wiki/History_of_education_in_the_United_States

51. Catherine Clinton, "Equally Their Due: The Education of the Planter Daughter in the Early Republic", Journal of the Early Republic 1982 2(1): 39–60

52. Lawrence Cremin, American Education: The Colonial Experience, 1607–1783 (Harper & Row, 1970)

53. https://en.wikipedia.org/wiki/History_of_education_in_the_United_States

54. Taken from "History of Boston Latin School—oldest public school in America" . BLS Web Site.

55. Taken from, The Mather School is marking 375 years of public education; NYPD's Bratton, an alumnus, to speak at assembly | Dorchester Reporter. www.dotnews.com

56. Jurgen Herbst, The Once and Future School: Three Hundred and Fifty Years of American Secondary Education (1996)

57. Paul Monroe, A Cyclopedia of Education (4 vol. 1911)

58. Hannah Barker and Simon Burrows, eds. Press, Politics and the Public Sphere in Europe and North America 1760–1820 (2002) p. 141

59. Lawrence A. Cremin, The Wonderful World of Ellwood Patterson Cubberley (1965)

60. Peterson, Paul E. (2010). Saving Schools: From Horace Mann to Virtual Learning. pp. 21–36. Messerli, Jonathan (1972). Horace Mann: A Biography

61. James McLachlan, American Boarding Schools: A Historical Study (1970)

62. Arthur Powell, Lessons from Privilege: The American Prep School Tradition (Harvard UP, 1998)

63. Ronald Story, "Harvard Students, The Boston Elite, And The New England Preparatory System, 1800–1870", History of Education Quarterly, Fall 1975, Vol. 15 Issue 3, pp. 281–298

64. Clark, Robenstine. "French Colonial Policy and the Education of Women and Minorities: Louisiana in the Early Eighteenth Century", History of Education Quarterly (1992) 32#2 pp. 193–211

65. Sol Cohen (1976) The History of the History of American Education, 1900–1976: The Uses of the Past. Harvard Educational Review: September 1976, Vol. 46, No. 3, pp. 298–330.

66. Taken from
    https://doi.org/10.17763/haer.46.3.gp631173780x51
    1j

67. Taken from, https://eric.ed.gov/?id=EJ152811

68. Jurgen Herbst, The Once and Future School: Three
    Hundred and Fifty Years of American Secondary
    Education (1996)

69. Peterson, Paul E. (2010). Saving Schools: From
    Horace Mann to Virtual Learning. pp. 21–36.
    Messerli, Jonathan (1972). Horace Mann: A
    Biography

70. Taken from, The Impact of the Factory Model of
    Education in Central Texas, abstract, Kelsey Leigh
    Stokes, Baylor University, 2013

71. Dewey, John (1916). Democracy and Education: An
    Introduction to the Philosophy of Education.

72. Peters, Michael. "Ecopolitical Philosophy, Education and
    Grassroots Democracy: The return' Of Murray Bookchin
    (and John Dewey?)". Geopolitics, History and
    International Relations, vol. 9, no. 2, Addleton Academic
    Publishers, July 2017, p 7

73. Taken   from,
    http://www.educationnews.org/education-policy-
    and-politics/american-public-education-an-origin-
    story

74. Jurgen Herbst, The Once and Future School: Three
    Hundred and Fifty Years of American Secondary
    Education (1996)

75. Plank, David N.; Peterson, Paul E. (1983). "Does
    Urban Reform Imply Class Conflict? The Case of
    Atlanta's Schools". History of Education Quarterly.
    23 (2): 151–173

76. Leuchtenburg, p 121–22; Tyack et al. Public Schools
    in Hard Times (1986) pp 105.

77. Kevin P. Bower, "'A favored child of the state':
    Federal Student Aid at Ohio Colleges and
    Universities, 1934–1943". History of Education
    Quarterly 44.3 (2004): 364–387.

78. Taken from, https://www.usnews.com/news/special-reports/articles/2014/02/27/the-history-of-common-core-state-standards

79. Refer to: http://www.corestandards.org/

80. Taken from http://www.wnd.com/2000/09/4581/, by Julie Foster, NEA vs. home schools Union opposes nearly every aspect of parent-directed education
Published: 09/10/2000 at 1:00 AM

81. http://www.wnd.com/2000/09/4581/

82. Refer to:
http://www.opensecrets.org/industries/indus.php?ind=L1300

83. http://www.wnd.com/2000/09/4581/

84. Refer to *The Eagle Forum*, The Phyllis Schlafly report website at:
http://eagleforum.org/publications/psr/aug15.html

In Closing

As **Classroom CPR** (Classroom Preparation and Revitalization), my wife and I are Education Consultants and Student Learning Advocates. In this, we accept speaking engagements and presentations on classroom management and student engagement and motivation. These activities and selling a series of books are what we get paid for. But parents and students sometimes need advice from an experienced professional; this advocacy is what we do not get paid for. It is a service at info@marisector.com or our website www.cpr4classroommanagement.com.

Please complete the self-assessment forms at the end of each chapter. Email them to the address shown above. Once we receive all 11, we will send a course completion certificate to present to your curriculum provider if requested. Also, we will send updated information to you to assist with your student's learning into the future. Watch for our chat line on our website.

Published Material

Jeffrey L. Kuhlman

Books Published:
  Concepts in Maritime Tactics
  Security for Recreational and Charter Yachts
  Awareness for Maritime Security and
  Basic Course in Maritime Security
  Shipboard Security Team Officer/Leader
  Firearms in the Maritime, Practical Tactics:

Curriculum Development:
6000 level at Nova Southeastern University:
  Maritime History
  Introduction to the Maritime Industry
  Maritime Safety and Security

Books in Publishing:
  Contributing author in *Research-Based Strategies to Grow Student Learning;* Chapter, *Education in Distressed Environments*
  Proposed, *Help for Home-Schooling in the Faith-Based Family*

Other Curricula:
  Maritime Security Team Officer
  Train the Disaster and Emergency Preparedness Trainer (In English and Spanish)

Articles:
Published Blog and accompanying videos,
www.rwt2015.com

10 Proven Steps to Effective Leadership
The Next Ten Steps to Effective leadership
Understanding Trump, 3/2017
Patio Chat #1 Estate System, 4/2017
Youth Suicide, Understanding and Help, 6/2016
Patio Chat #2 Words, 10/2016
Patio Chat #3 Economic Consideration, 10/9/2016
Captain Jeff's Fun and Easy History, Volumes 1–5, 7/2016

Contributing Author to:
Maritime Professional Magazine; *Journal of International Association of Counter-Terrorism and Security Professionals*; *Workboat Magazine*; *Marine Log*; and *The Triton*

When Is the Maritime Industry Going to Train Maritime Professionals?
Risk Management for Shipboard Defense
Considerations for Shipboard Security
Understanding the Real Threat
A Vessel Security Breath of Fresh Air?

Our own Education Consulting and Student Learning Advocacy, Classroom CPR, offers the following, with more coming available soon, training materials offered by The Kuhlmans presentation team and on-site instructors as Classroom CPR.

The materials available below can be purchased online at www.CPR4Classroommanagement.com or info@marisector.com for materials, presentations, and training.

Teach-To's: 100 Behavior Lesson Plans and Essential Advice
Helps students understand what is expected of them.

Time To Teach: Encouragement, Empowerment, and Excellence in Every Classroom
An excellent reference for the classroom teacher.

Time To Teach: The Source for Classroom Management
Training textbook. Only available at Time To Teach
training.

*Differentiated Instructional Strategies for Student
Motivation and Engagement*
This is a textbook only sold to persons taking or
Differentiated Instruction course.

*Differentiated Instruction: Engagement and Motivation in
Every Classroom*
Presentation of differentiated instruction techniques for
students on any subject.

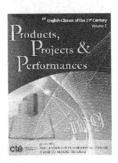

Differentiated Instruction for English
Projects for student motivation in the English language.

Differentiated Instruction for Mathematics
Projects for student motivation in mathematics.

Differentiated Instruction for Science
Projects for student motivation in science.

Differentiated Instruction for Social Studies
Projects for student motivation in social studies.

Time To Teach: Encouragement, Empowerment, Excellence
In Every Classroom. Audio Book. An excellent reference for
the classroom teacher.

Teachin' the Blues Away CD: Music designed to teach by.

Time To Teach: Encouragement, Empowerment, and Excellence in Every Classroom.
This is the complete course, less REFOCUS, on a single CD.

Humor is an Attitude
Humor for teachers and public speakers by educator and
humorist, Jim-Bob Solsbery.